RAND

Effective Use of Information Technology

Lessons about State Governance Structures and Processes

*Robert Anderson, Tora K. Bikson, Rosalind Lewis,
Joy Moini, and Susan Straus*

Prepared for Bureau of State Audits

RAND Science and Technology

The research described in this report was conducted by RAND Science and Technology for the Bureau of State Audits.

Library of Congress Cataloging-in-Publication Data

Effective use of information technology : lessons about state governance structures and processes / Robert H. Anderson ... [et al.].
    p. cm.
    "MR-1704."
    ISBN 0-8330-3426-X
    1. Information technology—Government policy—California. 2. Information technology—Government policy—United States—States. I. Anderson, Robert H. (Robert Helms), 1939–

JK8749.A8E34 2003
352.3'84'09794—dc21

2003009405

RAND is a nonprofit institution that helps improve policy and decisionmaking through research and analysis. RAND® is a registered trademark. RAND's publications do not necessarily reflect the opinions or policies of its research sponsors.

Published 2003 by RAND
1700 Main Street, P.O. Box 2138, Santa Monica, CA 90407-2138
1200 South Hayes Street, Arlington, VA 22202-5050
201 North Craig Street, Suite 202, Pittsburgh, PA 15213-1516
RAND URL: http://www.rand.org/
To order RAND documents or to obtain additional information, contact Distribution Services: Telephone: (310) 451-7002;
Fax: (310) 451-6915; Email: order@rand.org

Preface

The study reported here was undertaken because of questions being raised about the effectiveness of information technology (IT) governance in the State of California. Created in 1995 by the California legislature, the Department of Information Technology (DOIT) was to provide leadership, guidance, and oversight for IT initiatives and projects throughout the state. By the summer of 2002, DOIT would cease to exist, but the need for what DOIT was chartered to do would continue.

RAND, as an independent nonprofit research organization, responded to a request for proposals to conduct a study of California's IT governance structures and strategies for the Bureau of State Audits. The request for proposals resulted from legislation aimed at determining whether California's IT program complied with best practice and identifying any reforms needed. Between the time of the original legislative request and the awarding of the study contract to RAND, DOIT's sunset clause was allowed to take effect. The orientation of the study was therefore refined to emphasize how California could best take advantage of prior experience, both in that state and elsewhere, to shape future directions in IT governance.

This report is intended to inform and advise policymakers in the state of California about the next steps toward effective IT governance structures and processes. However, we believe the findings and recommendations will be of interest to a broader range of decisionmakers, stakeholders, and researchers concerned with how best to deploy advancing IT to serve public sector missions.

The project was housed within RAND's Science and Technology (S&T) research unit. Its charter is to assist government and corporate decisionmakers in developing options to address challenges created by scientific innovation, rapid technological change, and world events. RAND S&T's research agenda is diverse. Its main areas of concentration are science and technology aspects of energy supply and use; environmental studies; transportation planning; space and aerospace issues; information infrastructure; biotechnology; and the federal R&D portfolio.

Inquiries regarding RAND Science and Technology may be directed to:

Stephen Rattien, Director
RAND Science and Technology
1200 South Hayes Street
Arlington, VA 22202-5050
Phone: (703) 413-1100 x5219
Email: contact-st@rand.org
Website: www.rand.org/scitech/

Contents

Figures

Figures

Summary

In 1995, the California Department of Information Technology (DOIT) was created to provide leadership, guidance, and oversight for Information Technology (IT) initiatives and projects throughout the state. By 2002, DOIT would cease operation, but the need for what DOIT was chartered to do would continue.

California, the most populous state in the union, is governed by a multitude of agencies and departments each with a mission to support the business of the state. The complexity of the state's governance and other circumstances created challenges for DOIT as it attempted to achieve its mission. Some of these challenges can be traced to the composition and organizational placement of DOIT, others stem from the all-encompassing charter of being both an advocate and control organization, and still others are a result of the inability of state IT stakeholders to collaborate.

To determine what lessons can be learned from states with exemplary practices in IT governance, we conducted case studies in Virginia, New York, Pennsylvania, and Illinois. The studies surfaced three quite different models for achieving effective IT governance. They varied substantially in the extent to which formal authority is concentrated in the state's highest-level IT office as well as where that office is located in the governance structure and how it interacts with other stakeholders in IT initiatives.

Cross-case analyses plus a review of relevant research literature enabled us to identify a number of common factors likely to account for successful IT programs under different governance models. These include: (1) executive leaders who are champions of IT and emphasize its value for achieving state missions; (2) a management style that is participative and collaborative, that emphasizes "carrots" over "sticks," and that evidences a commitment to employees during periods of change; and (3) a modular and incremental approach to development and implementation of IT initiatives. These factors did not characterize California's approach to IT governance.

Besides common success themes, there are a number of common challenges faced by states, regardless of their approach to IT governance. Most of these challenges involve making decisions about tradeoffs among competing interests and approaches, with no particularly right answers. Among the most critical challenges is the need to determine the appropriate amount of centralization of state IT functions and the degree of standardization of IT systems. A related challenge is ensuring public values such as equity through competitive procurement when deciding on the degree of standardization. The decision whether to outsource IT operations poses a challenge for state government, which must weigh the benefits of the flexibility gained from contractor-provided services against developing overdependence on such services. In deciding on the appropriate strategic approach, states face a challenge in developing an IT strategic plan focused on IT, or developing a business strategy in which IT plays a supporting role. Another issue faced by state governments is the establishment of an IT inventory and a regular refresh cycle of IT office equipment, lessening the burden of the approval and procurement process requirements for such routine purposes.

Moreover, operating in the public sector poses some unique challenges that state governments must face in carrying out their IT operations. Critical decisions about the type of oversight for IT budgets and procurements must take into account the appropriate level of oversight to ensure accountability, while giving agencies enough flexibility and discretion to meet their IT needs. Another challenge unique to the public sector is the effect of administration turnover on the continuity of the statewide IT vision. In addition, the lengthy state government budget cycle causes major problems for IT development. The impending baby boom retirement also has major implications for the public sector because of its limited ability to hire enough personnel with the needed IT skills. Lastly, the importance of executive leadership for IT and the creation of a collaborative organizational culture are challenges that must be addressed, particularly in California.

We conclude that other states are providing visionary management, oversight, and control of major IT initiatives at the state government level in the face of such challenges. Those states' governance structures differ in the amount of authority given to an IT agency. Other states are consolidating state data centers, foreseeing a variety of advantages. In each of the states studied, there is direct support from the governor's office for critical statewide IT initiatives, which seems to be a key factor in their success. Themes arising from the operation of other states' IT agencies are promotion of a modular approach to IT developments, and the need to deal with complications arising from a yearly budget planning and approval cycle. Our California interviews lead to the conclusions that the former California DOIT was not sufficiently effective, and that leadership style appears to be a critical success factor. Part of the management style and context in other states' effective IT programs is use of IT

Figures

oversight and advisory boards, and widespread use of master service agreements and statewide license agreements. We also conclude that, since IT oversight and governance in California has now been reconsolidated within the Department of Finance, moving some of this authority to a new agency will involve significant power shifts, possibly resulting in compromises of the type that crippled the previous DOIT.

On the basis of lessons learned in other states, we recommend that a new agency of information technology be established for California, reporting directly to the Office of the Governor. Existing statewide IT data centers should report directly to this new agency, and the existing offices of e-government and IT innovation should be consolidated within the new IT agency. The technical parts of the existing Technology Investment and Review Unit (TIRU) and Technology Oversight Review Unit (TOSU) groups within Finance should also be transferred to the new IT agency. The key roles for the new IT agency involve advocacy of statewide IT initiatives, coordination of IT activities, and technical approval of major IT projects and procurements. The new agency should establish a context and management style conducive to success, including stress on modular development and early successes in IT projects and development of regular, collegial relations with Finance, the Legislature, and agency and department CIOs. It should be encouraged to establish advisory boards. The agency should also address change management issues, including specifically the treatment of state IT employees as new systems and skills are required and older ones become obsolete, as well as workforce issues related to the potential retirement of large numbers of the IT workforce within coming years. Developing effective governance structures and processes for the state's deployment and use of IT should be regarded as critical to California's vitality in the 21st century.

Acknowledgments

We are indebted to the staff of California's Bureau of State Audits for their assistance in developing and carrying out this research. They provided background reports and documents for state IT-related activities, facilitated contacts with numerous state agencies, and offered collegial support throughout the project. We especially want to recognize the efforts of Norm Calloway (Project Manager) and Doug Cordiner (Audit Principal) who painstakingly reviewed earlier drafts of this report.

We would also like to acknowledge several RAND colleagues for their contributions to the project. Special thanks go to Rachel Rue for her invaluable help with a review of recent journal literature and to Michael Woodward for his skillful preparation of project reports (many versions) and related documentation. Additionally, we are grateful to Edward Balkovich and J. D. Eveland for their insightful and timely reviews of the final manuscript.

Finally, we wish to thank the state agencies in California, Illinois, New York, Pennsylvania, and Virginia that took part in this study. Their representatives made time available to cooperate in the research, candidly sharing their knowledge and experience. We learned a great deal from them.

Acronyms

AIO	Agency Information Officer
BCP	Budget Change Proposal
BOE	Board of Equalization
BSA	Bureau of State Audits
Caltrans	California Department of Transportation
CCS	(Bureau of) Consolidated Computer Services
CIO	Chief Information Officer
CMAS	California Multiple Award Schedule
CMS	Central Management Services
COTS	Council on Technology Services
CTO	Chief Technology Officer
DGS	Department of General Services
DIT	Department of Information Technology
DMV	Department of Motor Vehicles
DOB	Division of the Budget
DOF	Department of Finance
DOIT	Department of Information Technology
DTP	Department of Technology Planning
ECO	Electronic Collections Online
EDD	Employment Development Department
ELA	Enterprise License Agreement
ERI	Early Retirement Initiative
ERIC	Education Resource Information Center
ERP	Enterprise Resource Planning
FSR	Feasibility Study Report
GIS	Geographic Information System
GSP	Gross State Product
HIPAA	Health Information Portability and Accountability Act
IPOC	Independent Project Oversight Consultant

IRM	Information Resources Management
IT	Information Technology
ITB	Information Technology Bulletin
ITEPS	Illinois Technology Enterprise Planning System
ITP	Intent to Procure
ITQ	Invitation to Qualify
IV&V	Independent Verification and Validation
J-NET	Pennsylvania's Justice Network
MSA	Master Service Agreement
OA	Office of Administration
OB	Office of Budget
OFT	Office for Technology
OGS	Office of General Services
OIT	Office of Information Technology
PAIS	Public Affairs Information Service
ROI	Return on Investment
SOIT	State Office of Information Technology
SPR	Special Project Report
TIP	Technology Investment Program
TIRU	Technology Investment and Review Unit
TOSU	Technology Oversight Review Unit
VIPnet	Virginia Information Providers Network Authority

1. Introduction to the Research

Purpose

In 1995 the California Department of Information Technology (DOIT) was created to provide leadership, guidance, and oversight for Information Technology (IT) initiatives and projects throughout the state. By 2002, DOIT would cease operation, but the need for what DOIT was chartered to do would continue. The overall goal of the research reported here is to advise state policymakers on how California can fulfill the as yet unmet need for effective IT governance in the service of state missions.

Overview

RAND, as an independent nonprofit public policy research institution, responded to a request for proposals to conduct a study of California's information technology governance structures and strategies for the Bureau of State Audits. The request for proposals resulted from legislation aimed at determining whether California's IT program complied with best practice, identifying any reforms needed, and reporting back to the Legislature by the end of February 2003.

Between the time of the original legislative request and the awarding of the study contract to RAND, DOIT's sunset clause took effect and it ceased operation. The orientation of the present study was therefore refined to emphasize how California could best take advantage of prior experience, both in this state and elsewhere, to inform the next steps to take in IT governance.

Objectives

The study reported here is organized around three key objectives:

- obtain an understanding of how California's IT governance structure worked to coordinate, evaluate, oversee, and exploit as fully as possible the state's investment in IT;
- determine what lessons can be learned from states with exemplary practices in IT governance; and

- make recommendations for future directions in California's IT program to support the state's missions in the years ahead.

To achieve these objectives, the study relied on a replicated case study design that has guided successful RAND research on factors that influence the effective implementation of information technology in varied public and private sector organizational settings.[1] Cases, for purposes of this research, comprise the entities, structures, and processes that make up state-level IT governance. They can be regarded as "replications" because similar criteria were used to select participating sites and stakeholders in IT governance, and because common data gathering procedures were employed across the sites to pursue the key research questions.

Methods

IT Governance

In order to get a picture of IT governance, for replicated case study purposes, we began by identifying three types of state agency functions according to their involvement with the technology:

- *control agencies*: entities with authority for state-level IT policymaking, technical or financial approval of IT initiatives, or procurement approval (e.g., departments of information technology, departments of finance, general services departments);
- *client agencies*: entities that are major users of IT in the course of carrying out their missions (e.g., motor vehicle departments, health or social service departments, employment departments); and
- *technical agencies*: entities providing IT operations or services to other agencies (e.g., data centers offering hosting services, or e-government offices supporting enterprise-wide government portals).

All such entities are assumed to be significant stakeholders in IT governance at the state level, regardless of where they are housed structurally. In some states, for instance, technical services are operated by a central IT department while in

---

[1]See for example, Botterman et al., 2000; Bikson, 1998; Bikson and Eveland, 1996; Bikson and Frinking, 1993; Stasz et al., 1991, 1990; Bikson et al., 1987; Bikson, 1986. We view case study as the most appropriate method for examining and interpreting ongoing processes in real world contexts—especially when the processes to be studied (approaches to IT governance) are not sharply separable from their contexts (e.g., the broader state government environment) and when the variables of interest are likely to outnumber the potential units of study. (For further discussion of this type of research design, see Yin, 1994; Hersen and Barlow, 1976; and Campbell, 1975.)

others they report to client agencies. Likewise, in some states, the highest-level IT office constitutes a cabinet-level department, while in others it is housed within some other entity. In this research, we sought to study representative agencies of each type, learning where they are located structurally and how they interact to carry out the varied processes (e.g., planning, approval, implementation, and the like) required to accomplish IT initiatives of significance. The case studies we conducted therefore focus on the roles and relationships among control, client, and technical entities with respect to IT governance structures and strategies.

Site Selection

California was the initial site of study, in order to satisfy the first key objective of the research. In California, a considerable number of stakeholder entities in each of the three categories took part in the study. To fulfill the study's second key research objective—learning lessons about successful IT governance from which California might benefit—we sought to select four to six other states. We relied on three criteria to make the selection.

- *population size*: Participating states should be large enough that they have to cope with problems of scale, scope, and complexity reasonably similar to those that face California in its efforts to deploy IT effectively to serve state missions. To meet this criterion, we considered for inclusion only the states ranking in the top population quartile (or, excluding California, 12 states).

- *maturity of the state-level IT agency*: States selected should have had a state-level IT governance structure in place long enough to yield lessons based on experience with implementation of significant technology initiatives. For this purpose, we limited our case studies to sites whose state-level IT office had been established prior to 2000 (or 7 of the 12 size-eligible states).

- *exemplary practices*: States should be eligible for selection only if there is evidence that their IT implementation practices have yielded successes worth emulating. We operationalized exemplary status in two ways: reputation for excellence among peers (by soliciting nominations from interviewees); and evidence of significant IT achievements (e.g., by reviewing state web sites for documentation of IT initiatives accomplished and IT awards received).

Using these criteria, we selected New York, Illinois, Pennsylvania, Virginia, and Massachusetts. All but Massachusetts agreed to participate (Massachusetts agencies indicated that activities associated with the November 2002 election would make site visits too difficult to schedule but they would have been willing to arrange for telephone interviews). The four states chosen for study range in population size from 3rd (New York) to 12th (Virginia); their highest-level IT agencies range in maturity from three years (Illinois) to six years (Pennsylvania). Systematic case-comparative information about the participating states as well as their exemplary practices is provided in Appendix A (exemplary practices are highlighted as well in Chapter 4).

Procedures

Semi-structured interviews with representatives of agencies in the three categories outlined above constituted the primary data gathering method. The interviews were guided by a written protocol to ensure that information relevant to the key research objectives defined above would be systematically collected across states and agencies. While a more detailed protocol was employed in California and more agencies of each type were included, the basic structure of the interview remained the same for all sites and stakeholder organizations. Within selected organizations, we asked to speak with individuals familiar with IT development and deployment from the perspective of that agency's functions.

Substantively, interviews aimed to get a picture of the state's formal IT governance structure, giving greatest attention to enterprise-wide or otherwise large-scale and significant projects. They also sought to learn about the de facto roles and relationships among control agencies as well as between them and client agencies or technical service entities (or both). Then the interviews turned toward process questions, probing the way typical stages in IT development are carried out—for instance, the planning of IT initiatives, approaches to technical and financial approval, procurement, implementation, and evaluation. The interviews closed with questions about what worked well and badly, what future steps might be taken to improve the way IT initiatives are realized, and what else the responding agency representatives thought we should learn from them.

Information gathered in interviews was supplemented by reviews of related agency documents and web materials. In addition, we reviewed recent published research literature on IT governance to help corroborate and extend findings from the replicated case studies (see Appendix D).

Analysis Approach

Replicated case study methods rely chiefly on two types of analyses—within-case and between-case—to generate their findings.

Within-case analyses examine each site separately, systematically documenting the variables of interest defined in the research protocol: where control, client, and technical services agencies are situated in the formal governance structure; how authority for IT initiatives is allocated among them; the processes that typify IT initiatives from initial planning and approval to implementation and evaluation; the outcomes achieved; and the accompanying management style.

The first key research objective is satisfied by findings from the within-case study of California described in Chapter 2 below as well as in Appendix B. Within-case findings from the other states are presented in some detail in Appendix A. For each state, an initial table provides information about the location in the governance structure of the highest-level IT office and summarizes the roles of that and other control agencies in the state's IT program. Then key observations about typical IT project procedures, management functions, and technology issues are presented. Establishing a common structure for reporting within-case analysis findings is intended to facilitate cross-case comparisons and contrasts (see below).

Between-case analyses next examine each of the main variables of interest across sites, looking first for patterns of similarity and difference among them and then for contextual and other interpretive information to help explain the patterns obtained. Explanatory material is drawn from the research literature as well as data gathered in interviews and from agency documents.

Between-case analyses are used to explore differences among governance structures and processes, generating three alternative models for effective IT programs from the exemplary states studied; these findings are reported in Chapter 3 below. Cross-case analyses also helped to elicit common success themes (see Chapter 4) and common challenges to be addressed in state IT governance (see Chapter 5). Even where marked contrasts emerged between states' governance structures, we observed shared practices associated with successful IT deployment. On the other hand, we identified a number of recurring challenges that states can address in varying ways to enable IT improvements. Taken together, Chapters 3, 4 and 5 fulfill the second major research objective.

The third key objective—setting out future directions for California's IT governance—is addressed by comparing and contrasting what was learned from cross-case study of exemplary states with California's experience during DOIT's tenure. The resulting conclusions and recommendations are presented in Chapter 6.

Organization of the Report

The remainder of the report is organized as follows. Chapter 2 discusses IT governance in California. After situating DOIT in the governance structure, it describes the specific processes by which IT initiatives were carried out, concluding with key observations about the organizational context. Chapter 3 then presents findings from within-case analyses of four other states from which California could learn lessons about IT governance. In particular, it provides accounts of how control agencies in each state divide but integrate roles and responsibilities both structurally and in process terms, concluding with cross-case comparisons.

Findings from Chapter 3 indicate that control structures are only a part of effective IT governance. Chapter 4 therefore identifies IT governance success themes that recur throughout the exemplary states studied, despite their quite different formal governance patterns. And it provides corroborative evidence from the literature review, lending confidence in the efficacy of the success themes surfaced by our interviews. Similarly, Chapter 5 identifies IT governance challenges that commonly recur and for which there are no single clearly successful responses; here the key to effectiveness is to address them in balanced and situation-appropriate ways. For ease of comparison, we categorize both the success themes (Chapter 4) and the challenges (Chapter 5) in three groups: state governance structure and organization as related to IT; roles and functions of a statewide IT agency; and management style and context.

Finally, Chapter 6 sets out the study's conclusions and recommendations, ordered into the same three categories. They are based on comparisons between the detailed account of California's IT governance (Chapter 2) and findings about IT governance drawn from other states and on the research literature (Chapters 3 and 4). To enable linking the conclusions with recommendations, and to show their relationships to findings about success themes and challenges, we have used a common numbering scheme in presenting the main points in Chapters 4–6.

2. California's Search for Effective IT Governance

The Department of Information Technology (DOIT), which was created in 1995 by the California legislature and began operations in June 1996, was the most recent attempt to organize IT governance at the state level. DOIT, like the preceding organization, emerged as a result of the state's inability to prevent costly IT project failures. Unlike its predecessor, when DOIT was created, it was set apart from the organization that had historically performed state IT governance. This distinction, and the fact that DOIT's charter included leadership, guidance, and oversight, led to several problems that plagued the new and unproven DOIT throughout its existence.

The Present Situation

California relies heavily on IT to execute the mission and services of the state. For example:

- Nearly all Department of Transportation (Caltrans) projects involve IT. Computers, networks, and sensors are critical in many areas such as: meters that monitor and synchronize freeway on/off ramps; bridge controls for pumps, ventilation systems, and drainage and traffic flow control systems.

- IT is a large part of the business objective for the Employment Development Department (EDD). EDD currently has initiatives to move into e-government for on-line filing of taxes. The impact of 9/11 on unemployment insurance has resulted in the need for many changes, to accommodate the increased volume for which the system was not originally designed.

- The Board of Equalization's (BOE) considers IT as the core of its business function rather than an administrative or service function solely.

The ability of these organizations to manage resources and deliver services to citizens is inextricably linked to an expectation of increased effectiveness and efficiency resulting from IT. IT is the heart of delivering many services in the state, and in an Executive Order dated July 1, 2002 (D-59-02), the governor states "information technology is an indispensable tool of modern government."

8

The former DOIT was chartered to provide leadership, guidance, and oversight of information technology in the state government. To achieve this mission, it was necessary for DOIT to interact and coordinate with the Department of Finance (DOF) and the Department of General Services (DGS) for control of the process. Likewise, it was necessary for DOIT to interact with the clients of this process, varied agencies and departments, to exchange information that enabled the control decisions and oversight strategies employed by this process. However, the governance under these arrangements suffered many challenges such as the lack of a strategic plan to guide IT project planning and approval, dual project approval authorities, and cumbersome oversight requirements. These contributed to a perception of ineffectiveness on the part of DOIT, which, when combined with highly public and adverse state IT contract negotiations, resulted in a lack of legislative support for the continued existence of the organization.

Thus, although the legislature had previously asked for a review of DOIT's practices aimed at identifying desirable reforms, it did not intervene to prevent a sunset clause from ending the agency's existence on July 1, 2002. At that point the governor gave back to departments and agencies primary responsibility for their IT activities. It also gave the Department of Finance (DOF) through its Technology and Investment Review Unit (TIRU) and its Technology Oversight Review Unit (TOSU) technical approval roles for state IT projects. DOF is currently developing and implementing an oversight framework, assessing the current management and oversight practices of departments, agencies, and industry to establish statewide best practices in this area, and handling other aspects of IT issues as they arise (Finance, 2002). DOF is also working on developing a security policy program, capitalizing on the knowledge and assets of state departments to form a security policy advisory group to establish new policies and procedures for IT security. Both the oversight and security plans will continue to develop over the coming months, with periodic updates published in budget and management memorandums.

An Advisor on Information Technology and Chief Information Officer (CIO) for the State of California was appointed on September 20, 2002. The purpose of the new "Advisor/CIO" position is to provide leadership on IT policy and collaborate with other IT leaders in state government. This action was taken in response to the closure of DOIT and the departure of the previous state CIO in June 2002. The current Advisor/CIO reports to the governor but does not have oversight or control responsibilities for state IT initiatives. In this report we do not assess present arrangements for IT governance. Rather, data collected about

California's governance structures and processes are bounded by the time period of DOIT's existence.

In what follows, we first describe the establishment of DOIT within the state's government structure. Then we examine the processes this new entity was intended to carry out. Two appendices supplement this discussion. Appendix B provides a list of the California organizations interviewed and summarizes key comments about DOIT's procedures and its management capabilities. Appendix C outlines recommendations for performance improvements made to DOIT in spring 2001 and gives indicators of the extent of progress made on each by the time of DOIT's closure a year later.

The Establishment of DOIT Within State Government

Both size and diversity are key factors that complicate the task of IT governance in the state of California. While other states may face similar challenges and opportunities, California is very different from other states in one key dimension. With 34.5 million residents, it ranks first in population, outnumbering the next biggest state, Texas, by approximately 13 million (U.S. Census Bureau, 2001). These residents are served by a complex architecture of agencies, departments, boards, and other organizational constructs that execute the mission of the state.[1] As noted earlier, the ability of these agencies to deliver mission-critical services increasingly depends on advanced IT. However, by the mid-1990s it was clear that California was not developing the kinds of governance structures and processes that would promote effective IT deployment.

DOIT was created in response to a number of costly and embarrassing problems with implementing various IT projects in California state agencies. The culmination of these failures was documented in three separate reports in 1994 which all found that there was insufficient statewide planning, coordination and leadership for IT (LAO, 1994; Task Force, 1994; BSA, 1994). In response, the California legislature held a series of hearings and passed legislation forming DOIT as an independent agency, with the state's Chief Information Officer designated by the governor as its director. (SB 1, Alquist, 1994).

Prior to the creation of DOIT, responsibility for IT oversight belonged to the Office of Information Technology (OIT) in the DOF. OIT was created in 1983 to

___
[1]Later in the text, this condition is referred to as the diversity of agencies and departments in California. The differences are due to varied reporting structures (some to the governor, some to elected boards), funding structures (general fund, special funds, federal dollars), IT staff sizes (ranging from 6 to 1000), and vastly differing missions.

replace the State Office of Information Technology (SOIT), also housed in *DOF*, with a purpose and mission that eventually would become the blueprint for DOIT. OIT was given the responsibility to develop plans and policies for the application and development of IT in the state, and for oversight of state agency IT projects. However, OIT was sharply criticized for failing adequately to perform these responsibilities after a number of costly IT project failures—most notably, the Department of Motor Vehicles database redevelopment project that cost the state $49 million and did not result in a working system. Audits by the Bureau of State Audits and reviews by the Legislative Analyst's Office and the Task Force on Government Technology Policy and Procurement regarding the state's IT programs prompted legislative hearings and the introduction of legislation to create a new department that would provide the badly needed leadership and oversight for the state's IT program.

In 1994, legislation was introduced to create DOIT. In its original form, the legislation included a provision for a cabinet-level CIO and would have transferred all of the former OIT personnel from DOF, and DGS personnel involved with IT acquisition into the new department, to be called the "Information Services Agency." It would have also consolidated the administration of the data centers under the new entity. The legislation did not pass in this form because of competing interests, and a revised bill (SB1) was approved by the legislature in October 1995 (Peterson, 2002). Some expressed concern over the modified bill, citing the major problem that key positions and power were retained by the DOF. While SB 1 transferred oversight responsibility to the new DOIT, DOF retained financial authority for IT projects in its newly created Technology Investment and Review Unit (TIRU).

DOIT was charged with "providing leadership, guidance, and oversight of information technology in state government" (SB 1, Alquist, 1994). Most of its responsibilities centered on developing plans and policies to support the effective use of IT. This included responsibilities to manage the acquisition and appropriate use of IT in state agencies, to coordinate between various federal, state, and local government stakeholders as well as private industry, and to ensure that agencies' IT plans and projects were in line with the state's vision and goals for IT. DOIT was also given direct oversight authority to review, change, or veto agencies' IT projects as it deemed necessary (SB 1).

Thus, from the very beginning of DOIT's existence, a number of problems threatened its ability to effectively operate in accordance with legislative intent within the state government structure as it was eventually configured.

DOIT's Roles in Key IT Deployment Processes

DOIT was initially chartered to provide "leadership, guidance, and oversight" of information technology in state government. Functionally speaking, the IT development processes were conceived in terms of the five steps in Figure 1.

RAND*MR1704-1*

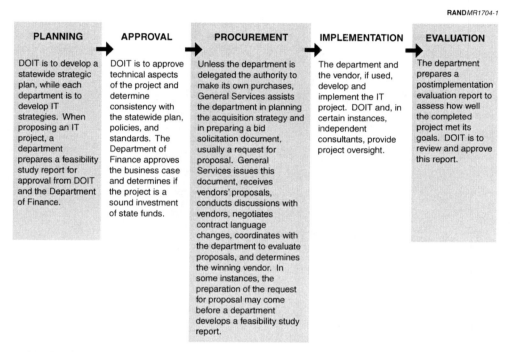

SOURCE: "Information Technology: The State Needs to Improve the Leadership and Management of Its Information Technology Efforts," BSA, June 2001.

Figure 1—California's Information Technology Development Process

We use this framework below to examine the roles DOIT played in IT development processes.

Planning

DOIT's responsibilities in the planning phase were primarily to collaborate and to advise. One problem DOIT faced was trying to balance this advocacy role with its control function. Another problem was that DOIT never quite established itself as a trusted and credible advisor.

In its collaborative role, DOIT tried to work with departments and agencies when project initiatives were being formed, a step that some thought beneficial to the development and subsequent review of a Feasibility Study Report (FSR).

Effective IT project definition requires consideration of the business objectives, which determine the requirements, and knowledge of and proficiency in the technology. Departments and agencies put significant emphasis on the up-front process to prepare a strong FSR. The nature of this up-front involvement, which DOIT was trying to become more involved in, is quite distinct from the remaining phases of the IT development process. The initial phase is focused on advocacy, while the latter phases focus on control.

In its advisory role, DOIT was supposed to develop a statewide strategic plan, which included revision of the statewide IT plan to address emerging critical IT issues as a result of recent administrative requirements. Subsequently, the statewide strategic plan would guide the development of department/agency IT plans and projects. However, due to California's size, diversity of department/agency priorities, and complexity of department/agency reporting structures this proved challenging. The process that DOIT used to update the strategic plan was not adequately inclusive of or responsive to department/agency CIOs, and the revision that was drafted, late in DOIT's existence, was neither well received nor complete. In some cases interviewees were unaware of its existence.

Approval

DOIT's role and responsibilities relative to other control organizations, in particular for approval, were not well defined or distinguished. SB 1 did not clearly state what roles and responsibilities DOIT would gain and what roles and responsibilities would be retained in DOF (via TIRU). It gave project approval authority to both DOF and DOIT. DOIT, DOF, and to some extent DGS all had a role in the approval process. In principle, DOIT was supposed to review the merits of the technology of a proposed IT project, while DOF would review the business case and approve funding, relying on DOIT's expertise to inform its decision. In practice, however, DOIT became primarily a "rubber-stamp" department, while DOF made the final decisions about IT project approval (LAO, 1996; interviews, 2002). Client agencies saw DOF and DOIT's roles as overlapping, even though there was no doubt that the final authority was with DOF. This ambiguity and imbalance of power eroded trust and confidence in these two control agencies from the client perspective.

DOIT's failure to produce an updated statewide strategic plan may have also contributed to another problem. Clients indicated that the approval process appeared preferential, arbitrary, and unilateral. For example, when a mission-critical prison IT system was denied by DOF, appeals to the administration overturned this decision because the outcome of not approving the system would have created unacceptable conditions in the prisons. The existence of a strategic plan may alleviate the problem of effectively disapproving (approve but not fund) or inadequately funding projects without consideration of multiyear effects, prior investment of resources, or overall mission objectives. This problem stems not only from a lack of direction that a strategic plan may provide, but also the apparent ability of DOF to exercise line item control (independently make specific cuts in funding or staff) over projects.[2] The statewide strategic plan (and related supporting plans) might have alleviated some ambiguity from approval process by serving as a guide to assess and judge projects. Frustration with the approval (and budgeting) process has motivated some clients to limit exposure to control phases of the IT development processes because they have become increasingly arduous and mired in mistrust.

Procurement

Of all the IT development process phases, DOIT's role in the procurement phase was the least prominent. However, DOIT was beginning to take on the task of leveraging the state's buying power (a task that many consider appropriate for a statewide entity), but in one particular incident this was not well executed. Legislative hearings accused DOIT of failing to review and assess the needs for a proposed statewide contract with the Oracle Corporation, which if executed, would have resulted in costly and unnecessary purchases of database software licenses for the state. As a result, for a brief period of time the California Multiple Award Schedule (CMAS), Master Service Agreements (MSAs), and Enterprise License Agreements (ELAs)—all vehicles to facilitate procurement and gain economies of scale for the state—were restricted, forcing more competitive bids and unraveling the state's buying power.[3] Managing the tension between statewide efforts for cost efficiency and effectiveness versus competitive procurements for equity and public trust was and will continue to be a significant challenge.

A related problem that DOIT faced was the definition and use of standards. Most agree that standards are needed and DOIT made some attempts to establish standards, but budgetary concerns regarding the cost impact on projects derailed such endeavors. Even had this not been the case, vendor lobbyists, who wield

---

[2]In response to this claim, Finance noted, "If we cut things we expect you to do a different project or justify the project."

[3]New guidelines for the use of these vehicles were issued by the Department of General Services in December 2002.

significant political power, may feel threatened and locked out of competition if standards (other than theirs) are set. DOIT's inability to make progress in this area contributed to a perception, by some, of ineffectiveness.

Implementation and Evaluation

DOIT's main role during these phases was oversight: reviewing project progress, assessing the resultant system, and when necessary redirecting or terminating a project. Highly publicized failures with political implications have evolved and expanded the oversight process with the objective of preventing the next troublesome project. As previously stated, DOIT was created with the explicit intent of providing leadership and guidance, as well as conducting oversight (a task that its predecessor allegedly did not satisfactorily perform).

Project oversight occurs at many levels both internal and external to departments/agencies, but there are varied opinions as to how much is necessary and where it should occur. DOIT initiated several strategies to fulfill its oversight responsibilities including the use of Independent Project Oversight Consultant (IPOC) and Independent Verification and Validation (IV&V) contractors. These extra personnel were usually at the expense of the department/agency because DOIT did not have the resources to undertake such an enormous task. The burden of meeting DOIT's oversight requirements was considered by some excessive, redundant, and at times trivial. In particular some felt that DOIT's oversight requirement for a department/agency should have been tied to the capability of the organization. On the other hand, some felt that independent oversight was an absolute must, because departments/agencies cannot effectively police themselves.

When asked, interviewees could not recall a specific incident where DOIT actually exercised its authority to terminate a project, possibly due to lack of influence or political support. Some interviewees suggested that DOIT did not have the real authority for oversight of projects, as requested by the Legislature (LAO, 1997).

A key challenge with DOIT's oversight role (and potentially any entity taking on this responsibility) is the definition of failure. When should a project be considered a failure? The operating definition is some predefined variance from the baseline in budget or schedule. Evidence from other domains suggests that this variance should be anticipated, partly because users are unable to fully anticipate or appreciate the impact of a new technology on their task or mission.[4] Additionally, other factors beyond the actual implementation of the project may contribute to these changes such as: control portions of the IT development process, the level of collaboration among stakeholders when the IT project spans organizational boundaries, and the dynamics of the state and its needs. Finally, the definition of "failed" may be misleading because failed projects often end up as useful systems. In California's context, "failed" projects include those that have generated adverse public headlines.

Other Problem Areas

Aside from the problems DOIT encountered with the IT development process, DOIT also faced a series of other problems related to the environment in which it operated. These problems originate from DOIT's structure and relationships with other organizations, as well as ambiguity in its role and function.

Organization and Support

California interviewees noted that in general SOIT, OIT, and DOIT all had similar constructs and similar challenges—namely, collaboration with and from other stakeholders in the process. Among the control organizations and client departments alike, a collaborative and supportive environment was at times lacking. As an example, interviewees cite DOF's reluctance to support DOIT's proposal for IV&V vendors, severely cutting the forecasted amount of contractor support needed for oversight.

According to the LAO, DOIT had neither the active support of the governor's office nor an adequate number of staff to carry out all the responsibilities it was given (LAO, 1999). DOIT was disadvantaged from the beginning, because none of the staff from the former OIT were permitted to transfer to the new department as it was established. DOIT thus lacked the institutional knowledge, particularly for control, from which to draw upon in carrying out its numerous responsibilities.

---

[4]In military information systems, studies suggests that early/static estimates for systems are often wrong. Specifically, it is "a faulty assumption . . . that users know what their requirements are, or at least should know. In fact, it is unreasonable to expect users to know, in any detail, what their requirements are or will be, when they do not have a full appreciation of the new or improved technologies, particularly in terms of implications for the environment or mission." Network Centric Warfare, http://www.dodccrp.org/Publications/pdf/ ncw_2nd.pdf.

Roles and Functions

DOIT received intermittent support from the governor. Two highly successful initiatives—the Year 2000 conversion effort and the My California Web Portal project—enjoyed the public backing of the governor, but IT initiatives in general received little attention from the administration (Little Hoover Commission, 2000). DOIT received high praise for its role in the California Year 2000 conversion effort. It was credited with providing strong leadership and identifying and acting on problems early, in collaboration with state agencies. On the other hand, DOIT was minimally involved in the My California Web Portal project, and this dispersion of IT responsibilities was seen by some as a lack of confidence in DOIT's ability.

However, DOIT's presence as a statewide IT organization may have created inconsistent and unrealistic expectations. California interviewees identified several roles they thought appropriate for a statewide entity. These included items such as responsibility for ubiquitous functions, responsibility to advance initiatives from an enterprise-wide perspective and the provision of a community forum to address common issues. DOIT attempted to do all of these. It tried to set policy and standards for security, it tried to conduct enterprise licensing, and it tried to establish a community forum (CIO meetings) for sharing. All of these were less than successful, possibly because DOIT attempted to tackle too many challenges at once, rather than establish a set of priorities and tackle only the most important issues and challenges, as time and resources permitted.

Lastly, the manner in which DOIT approached these challenges did not always (from the client perspective) seem very collaborative. CIOs felt that DOIT did not consider or listen to what the departments and agencies needed in terms of standards and best practices. Rather, they felt that DOIT mandated many requirements and issued policy without using appropriate feedback and involvement of the clients. In its relationships with both control and client organizations, DOIT sometimes found itself at odds with other IT stakeholders.

Still Searching for an Answer

There still exists an unsatisfied need for IT governance in California. DOIT and previous governance structures (OIT, SOIT) fell out of favor when they unsuccessfully negotiated public and politically damaging IT development initiatives. Yet after several organizational attempts to structure IT governance and numerous studies on the challenges of governing IT in California, the state is still searching for an answer on how to govern IT. Given that IT is a core component of effective government and IT is recognized as critically important, why has IT governance been so problematic? It is instructive to review the conditions under which governance is attempted.

The application of IT in California is significant; it permeates nearly all aspects of state government. It is multifaceted, supporting a plethora of missions, and it is evolving in response to new and on-going needs. The stakeholders include Californians at the individual citizen level as well as private and public sector organizations. It encompasses individual citizens expecting a public good or service from the state and industries seeking business-friendly opportunities via efficient interaction in and with the state. It includes public institutions empowered to provide services for the public good, as well as the executive leadership of the state who are responsible for making decisions that will enhance and improve the state, where possible through the use of IT.

It is highly plausible that under the previously employed governance model, DOIT was neither appropriately defined nor adequately structured to account for the complexity of this task. Like its predecessors, it emerged in response to a perceived failure of the system to protect the investment of the state in IT. Unlike its predecessor, it reported to the governor's office, instead of an administrative department, and was headed by a state-level CIO. If the governance model is important, what other models are appropriate and would they work given California's situation? If the solution is greater than the governance model, what other factors contribute to successful IT governance? It is questions such as these that this present study was meant to address.

The following chapter describes our search for alternative models for state IT governance. Our research methods included criteria for selecting the other states whose governance structures we examined; development of a protocol to conduct interviews within those states; and a between-case analysis of the resulting data to generate three general models of IT governance.

3. Alternative Models of Effective IT Governance

Case studies of four exemplary states—Virginia, New York, Pennsylvania, and Illinois—surfaced three quite different models for achieving effective IT governance. The models differ most notably in the extent to which formal authority for IT governance is concentrated in the state's highest-level IT office. In Virginia, for instance, a great deal of responsibility for IT activities, ranging from policy development and enforcement to project technical approval and technical services operations, resides with its cabinet-level Technology Secretariat. In Illinois, by contrast, the state's Chief Technology Office has no formal governance authority; housed within the office of the governor, it acts chiefly by making recommendations to the governor and, through him, to the cabinet. These differences notwithstanding, the states studied have highly successful IT track records.

Three Governance Models

As explained in the Introduction to this research, a primary objective was to learn lessons about effective IT governance from other states' experiences. For this purpose we chose four states with reasonably large populations and relatively mature IT governance offices (like California) and with track records of successful IT initiatives (unlike California). The first lesson we learned is that effective IT governance at the state level can be achieved under widely varying structural and procedural arrangements. Between-case analyses of the four states we selected yielded three distinct models that differ markedly in where the highest-level state IT office is located structurally as well as the nature and extent of its influence over major IT initiatives relative to other stakeholders.

Below we first set out, for the states exemplifying these models, the mission and structural location of the highest-level state IT office as well as its main reporting relationships. Then we provide more detailed accounts of its technical control responsibilities (e.g., strategic planning, policy formulation, standards development, enterprise-wide project oversight or evaluation, and so on) as well as its technical operations (e.g., operating or directing the operation of data centers, e-government facilities, networks and telecommunications, security procedures, and the like). Finally, we give special attention in the discussion of each model to how technical authority and financial authority are coordinated in IT project approval processes.

We do not, of course, mean to suggest that this set of three models exhausts the options for effective IT governance; a study broader in scope might well have surfaced a larger set of models from which to draw lessons. Nonetheless, we believe the obtained set is sufficiently varied on the dimensions of research interest for purposes of this study to provide the ground for highly useful comparisons and contrasts. (Appendix A provides additional systematic comparative information from the case study sites.)

Consolidated Control: Consolidating Authority for Many Control Functions in the Central IT Office

In Virginia and New York, a great deal of authority for diverse aspects of the state's IT program is concentrated in a central high-level office. There are, however, some differences between them in how this authority is structured.

Virginia's highest-level office is its Technology Secretariat, headed by a cabinet-level secretary. The Technology Secretariat has two distinct but complementary goals: to enable IT to become a means for promoting economic development in Virginia's private sector; and to ensure that IT deployment in the public sector serves to improve the performance of the Commonwealth's missions. In fulfilling the latter aim, the Technology Secretary acts as the Chief Information Officer (CIO) for the Commonwealth. The case study emphasized the CIO-related functions of the Technology Secretariat.

Four technology-related departments report to the CIO, along with two advisory bodies: a CIO council, constituted by CIOs of private sector organizations, that gives advice on emerging new technologies; and a Council on Technical Services (COTS), comprising CIOs from varied client agencies at local as well as state levels, that advises on new opportunities to deliver improved services through technology. In the Secretariat itself, two of the departments take on significant control functions.

- The Department of Technology Planning (DTP) is responsible for preparing a centralized IT strategic plan along with related policies, guidelines, and standards (over which the Technology Secretary has final approval). Agency projects and enterprise-wide projects are approved only if they are consistent with these. DTP also has a role in project management and oversight. It has prepared standardized project management techniques, offers client agencies training and mentoring, and requires their use. After project contracts are signed, DTP engages in oversight and has the capability to "pull the plug" if a project is failing.

- The Department of Information Technology (DIT), in contrast, is operational in orientation. It is responsible for all data processing that requires mainframe applications; it also provides technical support for other databases, infrastructure operations, networks, and the security of all back-end processes. DIT additionally has responsibility for defining IT-related procurement policies. DIT itself handles all IT procurements over $50,000; under that level, client agencies are authorized to make their own purchases (consistent with DIT's policies). Non-IT procurements are handled by Virginia's Department of General Services (DGS).

The Technology Secretariat has no direct role in budgeting, apart from the ability to support some enterprise-wide projects with a limited Capital Fund. Generally, IT projects approved by DTP are prioritized and forwarded to the Office of Budget along with prioritized project requests from all the other cabinet secretaries. The Office of Budget is concerned strictly with dollar amounts requested and how to finance them. It accepts technical approval decisions made by DTP and tries not to cut funding requests so as not to jeopardize projects' success prospects; it never makes line item cuts but it may make alternative financing recommendations. The Office of Budget's recommendations then go to the governor, who makes final budget decisions.

In New York, by contrast, the Chief Information Officer is housed within the Office of the Governor and reports directly to him but it is not a cabinet-level position. Rather, that office was created by an executive order of the governor. The Office for Technology (OFT) is a separate agency that was created by the legislature but reports to the CIO. Other IT-related agencies that are not a part of OFT (e.g., the Geographic Information Systems (GIS) Office and the Office for Cyber Security) also report to the CIO. Additionally, the state CIO is served by two advisory bodies: the CIO Advisory Council (comprising private sector CIOs who give feedback on proposed new technologies); and the Architecture Board (which represents stakeholders in enterprise-wide systems). Roles are divided between the CIO's Office and OFT in ways that resemble the division of responsibilities between DTP and DIT in Virginia.

- The CIO has broad powers to develop and enforce IT policies and strategic plans. Agencies must prepare strategic plans that are consistent with the state plan and reflects its directions and priorities; and they are not allowed to make IT purchases until their plans are approved by the CIO. The CIO also decides on standards for basic platforms and enterprise-wide technologies. Presently, for instance, there is a moratorium on agency acquisition of financial management systems; because so many agencies have made requests to move to upgrade their old financial management technology, the CIO and OFT are pursuing a standard or guideline in this area.

- OFT, like DIT, has operational responsibilities. It has operational authority for the data centers as well as for telecommunications and networks (including e-commerce and e-government as well as data transfers involving private health information governed by the Health Information Portability and Accountability Act (HIPAA). Further, OFT has developed a project management guide and trains and mentors client agencies in this area. If client agencies want to use centralized Technology Entrepreneurial Funds for projects, they have to comply with the project management guidelines. Finally, OFT handles IT procurement when many or all agencies will be involved. It reviews smaller procurement requests for consistency with planned or existing tools and platforms (and looks for trends in new acquisitions). After OFT approval, these kinds of purchases are handled by New York's Office of General Services (OGS); but OFT also has to approve contractual arrangements with vendors.

Except for the capability to seed promising IT projects with the Technology Entrepreneurial Fund, the CIO and OFT do not have financial authority. Rather, that authority belongs to the Office of Budget. Early in the planning process, client agencies meet with Budget Office representatives to describe and justify their IT aims for the coming year. They get a fast response to their plans before preparing and submitting a full request. The Office of Budget does a review of the business case for IT that is independent of the technical review and makes funding decisions (although projects cannot be funded if they do not receive technical approval as well). Because of the early vetting process, client agencies' funding requests are usually approved by the Office of Budget.

Both New York and Virginia, then, concentrate a significant degree of control over IT policy, planning, and standards, as well as technical operations and procurement authority, in their highest-level IT organization. Within that organization, both divide major roles among constituent entities so that some are predominantly engaged with IT strategies and policy guidance while others have more hands-on responsibilities (e.g., operations, procurement). In both cases, these entities also control a limited central fund for stimulating new enterprise-level IT ventures. While financial authority in the main is formally retained by a finance or budget department, technical approval is required before a project can be funded. And when proposed IT projects are aligned with state priorities and judged to be technically sound, their funding requests are rarely denied. Future directions for both states include steps toward greater centralization and concentration of IT authority.

Collaborative Leadership: Institutionalizing Strong Collaborative Control Relationships Between the Central IT Office and Other Stakeholder Entities

In Pennsylvania, authority for the Commonwealth's deployment of IT is distributed among multiple departments and agencies. The effectiveness of this approach to IT governance depends on clear articulation and constructive integration of their separate roles.

The highest state-level office, the Office of Information Technology (OIT), is one of two major branches of the Office of Administration (OA), a cabinet department. The state CIO, as deputy secretary for OA, reports to the secretary, who in turn reports to the governor. Five regular divisions within OIT report to the CIO, along with Project Boards (enterprise-wide IT projects are overseen by specially constituted boards comprising representatives of the agencies involved). Additionally, all agency CIOs have a "dotted line" relationship to the state CIO even though they formally report to their own agency heads; they meet quarterly with him. The CIO also has an advisory CIO council whose members are CIOs in the private sector; they serve as a sounding board for exploring the potential of contemplated new enterprise-wide ventures.

- IT strategic plans, policies, standards, and guidelines are developed by the CIO with assistance from his policy and planning division. New policies and guidelines are issued first as draft IT Bulletins to all agencies, which have two weeks to respond with comments. After the comment period, the Bulletin is issued in final form and becomes binding. Agency-specific IT projects are initiated and planned by client agencies themselves, but must be compliant with OIT's standards and guidelines as well as with the Program Policy Guidelines issued by the governor's office. Concept plans and draft budgets for IT initiatives are submitted to both OA and the Office of Budget (OB), another cabinet-level department, for early feedback, with detailed plans and budgets to follow. Technical approval authority resides with OA while financial approval must come from OB. Enterprise-wide initiatives may be generated by OIT or may arise from the bottom up when multiple agencies submit concept plans reflecting shared needs.
- Besides policy authority and technical control, OIT has considerable operational responsibility. For instance, its bureau of consolidated computer

services led the centralization of 23 independent data centers into a single operation which the bureau now outsources but oversees. Its bureau of desktop computing selects, maintains, and upgrades a standardized suite of desktop tools across the Commonwealth's agencies. Other divisions are responsible for network and telecommunications policy and management as well as e-government planning and support. Additionally, OIT is responsible for managing enterprise-wide projects, with formal guidance from agency representatives. Project board members are able to vote on major project decisions; each agency on the board, regardless of size, has one vote. At the request of OB, OIT may also oversee and evaluate very large agency-specific IT projects.

Officially, OIT has no financial control over IT initiatives except through its Technology Investment Program (TIP) funds, which it uses to stimulate and reward innovative agency applications that have the potential to diffuse to other organizations in the Commonwealth. Formally, only OB has the authority to approve budgets. However, along with its technical review, OIT also examines budget requests associated with agencies' proposed projects and makes funding recommendations to OB. While these are advisory in nature, in practice OB usually concurs.

A third cabinet-level department, the Department of General Services (DGS), has formal responsibility for statewide procurement policies and procedures. DGS manages all hardware procurement, handling major acquisitions itself while allowing agencies to do small acquisitions (selecting from list of pre-qualified vendors and employing standardized purchase agreements). DGS delegates procurement of routine IT services to OIT; through its Invitation to Qualify (ITQ) process and its standard terms and conditions, OIT enables agencies to acquire these kinds of services on their own. Procurement of large-scale software systems and major systems integration services is also delegated to OIT; while OIT manages these acquisitions, DGS assists in developing and reviewing the bids and contracts.

As this overview suggests, Pennsylvania's IT governance relies on the sharing of authority among diverse stakeholders. OIT, for instance, formally empowers client agencies to share control over the development and implementation of the enterprise-level projects that will affect them. DGS delegates a substantial part of its IT procurement authority to OIT. And the Budget Office seeks and values the IT funding recommendations made by OIT while retaining official financial control. What makes this distribution of power effective, rather than crippling or divisive, is the close collaborative relationships that are cultivated by the stakeholders. Mutual respect, plus frequent and open communication and consultation, are cited as major contributors to Pennsylvania's success.

Advocacy: Establishing a Strong Advocacy Role for a Central IT Office That Does Not Have Formal IT Control Functions

In Illinois, the state's highest-level IT office has no formal governance authority. It achieves its effectiveness by playing a strong advocacy role; in the service of that role it acts as a change agent and brokers relationships among other key IT stakeholders.

The position of Chief Technology Officer (CTO) for Illinois was created by an executive order of the governor; it reports to the governor's office but is not a cabinet-level post. However, as a member of the governor's senior staff, the CTO has direct access to him and sits in on all cabinet meetings as well. Because it is not an independent department, the Technology Office does not have to compete with other departments to win support for its plans and priorities. On the other hand, all its authority derives from the governor. To get IT initiatives accomplished, the CTO makes recommendations to the governor, who then directs the cabinet to act on them. A Board of Advisors made up of CIOs from the client agencies in turn provides advice and feedback to the CTO.

- The Technology Office is charged with recommending IT standards and enterprise-wide IT initiatives; strategic planning for IT, however, is subsumed under the state's overall strategic plan, prepared by the Strategic Planning Office within the Bureau of the Budget (a cabinet-level department). Client agencies develop proposals for agency-specific applications, which are forwarded to the CTO for guidance. But final technical approval lies within the Office of Planning and Performance Review, also housed within the Bureau of the Budget.

- Most IT-related operational responsibilities are borne by the Central Management Services (CMS) department. Consolidated data centers, for instance, report to CMS. CMS is also in charge of IT procurement. It has established master contracts with vendors, which work well for hardware purchases and for maintenance service but are less successful for software acquisition; all systems programming services as well as systems integration have to be selected through a bidding process overseen by CMS. However, responsibility for carrying out enterprise-wide initiatives may be delegated to the CTO. For instance, the CTO was responsible for agencies' compliance with Y2K requirements, and now all IT components of Homeland Security initiatives have been delegated to the CTO. It is likely that compliance with HIPAA regulations will become the CTO's responsibility as well.

In the main, financial approval for IT projects rests with the Bureau of the Budget. However, there is a general Innovations Fund on which agencies may draw to cover project initiation costs if the CTO approves; these funds allow agencies to get off to a fast start on approved projects, partially offsetting some of the delay typically associated with lengthy government planning and budgeting lead times.

The main work of the CTO is done through communication, coalition-building, and coordination. For instance, the CTO has been able to broker some partnerships between the Budget Bureau, CMS, and client agencies to facilitate major IT projects. And it has established a good working relationship with the House Technology Committee. Additionally, the CTO has negotiated with CMS to arrive at some legal compromises between the need for technology standards on the one hand and the need for fairness on the other, in order to streamline time- and resource-intensive bidding processes. Finally, the CTO has organized several ongoing outreach and education activities, including: internal IT "fairs" where client agencies come together to share best practices; an internal seminar series to promote networking as well as professional development; and "Tech Town," an exhibit hall at the annual state fair where agencies set up booths to demonstrate to the public how IT is used in government.

Illinois' long list of accomplished enterprise-level IT projects is impressive given the Technology Office's relatively short history. It attributes its success to a governor who understands the power of IT for delivering services to citizens and for changing the way government agencies operate. Another key to getting IT done, according to the CTO, is having stakeholders who are committed, passionate, really willing to collaborate, and who do not give up on the shared goal of using IT effectively to perform state missions.

As is evident, case studies of the four exemplary states surfaced three quite different models for achieving effective IT governance. The models range widely in the degree to which formal authority for IT governance is concentrated in the state's highest-level IT office. Yet, regardless of differences in where they are situated in the governance structure and in their degree of formal power, all four of the state-level IT offices we studied played substantial roles in technical control areas and in varied technical operations. And, while none had significant financial control, each had a number of procedures in place for coordinating technical and budgetary approval of IT initiatives. Moreover, despite major differences in governance models, the states we studied have highly successful IT track records. It is likely that factors beyond formal governance structures and processes account for their positive IT outcomes. In the chapter that follows, we present success themes, identified in cross-case analyses, that contribute to effective IT governance.

4. Success Themes

The previous chapter shows three distinct IT governance models in use by the four non-California states studied. Clearly, any particular model is not a critical determiner of state IT governance success. But what then are such determiners? We asked ourselves, "What are the 'success factors' that allow some other states' IT initiatives to succeed, and the absence of which may well have contributed to the failure of the former DOIT?" We attempted to identify factors for success from the literature and our interviews so that whatever IT governance mechanism California adopts in the future might be designed explicitly with these characteristics in mind. Factors from the literature are based on empirical studies of IT or business processes. Factors from interviews were included only if they were mentioned by multiple respondents in each state.

Based on these sources of data, we uncovered a number of factors that contribute to the success of IT governance. These include: executive leadership support for IT, using a collaborative management approach, showing commitment to employees during periods of organizational change, and designing and implementing IT initiatives in modular form. These factors focus largely on organizational processes rather than technical specifications, policies, procedures, or standards. This emphasis reflects a recurring theme we heard from interviewees: that the technology part is easy; it's the organizational part that is difficult. Moreover, studies based on sociotechnical systems theory (e.g., Trist & Bamforth, 1951) confirm the importance of having good organizational/social *and* technical processes for effective performance. Such factors can enable successful IT governance independently of the degree of control vested in a state's highest IT office.

We elaborate on each of the success factors we believed were common in the states studied and of substantial importance, below. In this and the two following chapters we discuss success themes, challenges, and conclusions and recommendations within three overall topic areas:

1. Governance structure and organization of statewide functions

2. Roles and functions of a statewide agency

3. Management style and context.

It is our intent that, from this structure, the reader can follow our derivation of conclusions and recommendations from success themes and challenges in each of those topic areas.

1. Governance Structure and Organization of Statewide Functions

One organizational theme for statewide IT governance stood out in our study. We label this success theme S1.1, below.

S1.1. Success for Statewide IT Governance Is Enhanced by a Direct Reporting Relationship to the Governor's Office

As will be emphasized below (see S3.1), executive support for IT is critical. One way to demonstrate this support is through the organizational structure for IT governance. For instance, in Virginia, the Secretary of Technology is a cabinet-level position. Some interviewees stated that this structure communicates the message that the position has significant authority. In Illinois, the Chief Technology Officer sits within the governor's office and reports directly to him. Interviewees reported that having this special status with direct access to the governor, but not being at the same level as and in competition with other cabinet-level departments for resources and attention, was a major advantage. In New York, although the CIO position sits outside the governor's office, the governor issued an executive order establishing the CIO position and its powers. The research literature also supports the importance of having top-level champions of IT. In studies at the local and county levels, researchers have found that management support and leadership had a direct, positive influence on the commitment of employees to IT projects, organizational performance after IT implementation, and the realization of expected benefits from IT projects (Brown, O'Toole, & Brudney, 1998; Heintze & Bretschneider, 2000). A study of Fortune 1000 companies and government agencies found a significant positive relationship between top management leadership and the sophistication of IT infrastructure (Ravichandran & Rai, 2000). Other studies in the private sector have found that senior management support, championship, and commitment are critical for IT assimilation (Armstrong & Sambamurthy, 1999), for meeting procurement goals in large organizations (Avery, 2001), and for successful implementation of IT security (Internal Auditor, 1997). In fact, research on organizational change shows consistently that top management support is critical to the success of change efforts or other organizational initiatives, whether the initiatives are generated from the top down or bottom up.

A factor that contributes to placing value on IT is having executive leadership that understands the technical aspects of IT as well as good business processes. The Pennsylvania CIO is a superb example of a state IT leader who embodies these attributes. Through his experience in management positions in state government, both in IT and other aspects of business, the CIO has gained the knowledge of how IT can help the internal operations of the Commonwealth and provide services to its citizens. Likewise, in Virginia, the governor and CIO have substantial previous experience in the IT industry, which has enabled them to recognize how IT can improve business practices in the state. In fact, several interviewees in Virginia commented that the current governor and CIO "get it" when it comes to IT. Having a CIO and governor who "get it" not only contributes to the development of sound IT practices, but it enhances the leaders' credibility, which, in turn, engenders needed support from staff.

A focus on IT also depends on support from the legislature. In Pennsylvania, for instance, the CIO has good relationships with members of the legislature. Consequently, they support many of his recommendations. Similarly, in Illinois, the CTO has a very strong working relationship with the House Technology Committee, which has served the office well. Both states consider the support and understanding of IT by the legislature to be an important component of their success. In contrast, several respondents in Virginia and New York commented that members of their legislature do not understand IT and view it as a cost. Some in Virginia also commented that current or future legislation might make it difficult to implement the strategic IT plan by restricting the power of the Secretary of Technology's office. Whereas their CIO and governor work together effectively, it was not clear that they have such relationships with members of the state House or Senate.

2. Roles and Functions of a Statewide Agency

Two success themes relate to the roles and functions of a statewide agency: commitment to employees (those within the agency itself, as well as IT professionals in other state agencies); and emphasis on a modular approach to system development and procurement.

S2.1. States with Successful Information Technology Initiatives Demonstrate Commitment to Employees During Major Changes

One role of a statewide IT agency is to provide substantial career paths for IT professionals within the agency itself, and to aid in providing such paths for IT professionals in other state agencies. In concert with a collaborative approach (see S3.2, below) we found leaders who demonstrate a commitment to their employees' jobs and career opportunities in states with exemplary IT practices. There are several examples from Virginia. For instance, in Virginia, although the DMV was initially opposed to the directive to use VIPnet, executive leadership jumped on board and used the situation as an opportunity to restructure the department and make it more efficient. The DMV also retrained employees, allaying fears about layoffs across the state. When the Department of Taxation began its public/private partnership with AMS, the commissioner explained to employees that the change was not about cutting jobs and that all employees were needed to make the project work. Employees were flexible, took on new roles, took advantage of opportunities to learn by working side-by-side with AMS staff, and ultimately became owners of the project. When SAP workflow software was implemented in the Department of Corrections, the CIO used involvement, cross-training, and open communication that emphasized that employees would not lose their jobs. Similarly in Pennsylvania, when the OIT decided to consolidate 23 independent data centers into one, it made a commitment to train and redeploy personnel who would be displaced by the consolidation. The OIT followed through on this promise, which strengthened its credibility as an entity that keeps its word. A number of interviewees commented that through restructuring and retraining, employees gained opportunities to learn new skills. These efforts also freed up personnel to take on new projects, enabling the agencies to accomplish more of their IT objectives.

S2.2. Using a Modular Approach to Enterprise Initiatives Has Numerous Benefits

Another success factor cited by many of our interviewees is use of a modular approach to development and implementation of IT initiatives. Pennsylvania uses a concept referred to as an "energy burst development process," which was borrowed from an e-trade company. In short, it designs projects in modules in which benefits are delivered every 90 days. It can stop the full project and still have fully functional pieces with only three months of risk. This process shows value in a short time, and the ability to demonstrate results fosters subsequent employee motivation and support. A specific example from the Commonwealth is PA Open for Business, the web portal for small business owners (see http://www.paopen4business.state.pa.us/). The Commonwealth added a new piece to the website every 90 days until it became fully interactive. In 1995, Pennsylvania was one of only three states that did not have such a website; in 2001, it earned second place in Government Technology's annual, prestigious "Best of the Web" competition.

This modular approach also applies to the way in which initiatives are rolled out. For instance, the Pennsylvania portal was initially rolled out to a few key agencies. Agency heads talked to each other, which eventually led to a critical mass of participants.

We also saw examples of this approach in Virginia within specific agencies. For instance, the Department of Taxation undertook a large IT initiative to reengineer its tax collection processes four years ago including centralization of functions such as scanning, customer service, call center operations, and executive offices. It began by replacing all the existing software with new technology to support reengineered processes in imaging and scanning, followed by an Internet initiative and a customer relations initiative, accounting system changes, and an electronic collections system. It planned to close nine district offices, and began by closing two of them to show that it was effective. Auditors and collectors work from home or go to other agency offices for services such as teleconferencing. Ultimately, all 250 audit personnel will be mobile. The department decided to implement all of the customer-facing tools first, then the employee-facing tools, and last, the back-end system. It wanted to make small infrastructure improvements that could impact stakeholders. The Department of Corrections also uses incremental steps to change, and reports that successes encourage employees to continue their efforts.

3. Management Style and Context

Two management factors stood out in our interviews: knowledgeable executive support, and a collaborative management style.

S3.1. Executive Leadership Support for and Knowledge of Information Technology is Essential for Success

States with exemplary IT practices have executive leadership (governor and state CIO) who are champions of IT initiatives. All four of the states we visited exemplify this characteristic. These leaders emphasize the value of IT for the state in performing its missions. They view IT as an investment, rather than a cost, and they focus on using IT to provide services for citizens (rather than emphasizing return on investment (ROI), for instance). Indeed, empirical research in the public sector concludes consistently that IT investment pays off. Studies at local, county, state, and federal levels show that public sector IT investment has a direct, positive effect on productivity and performance (Brown, 2001; Brown, O'Toole, & Brudney, 1998; Heinze & Bretschneider, 2000; Lee & Perry, 2002; Lehr & Lichtenberg, 1996, cited in Lee & Perry, 2002). A study of IT investment by state governments, based on data from all 50 states, showed a direct, positive effect on economic productivity, as measured by Gross State Product (GSP). This held true whether IT investment was measured in financial terms or by a performance index based on total computer processing power (Lee & Perry, 2002).

Support for IT from state governors and CIOs is demonstrated in concrete ways. First, IT is an important part of the administration's agenda. The governors in the four exemplary states have clearly articulated goals for the use of IT in their states that are well known to the rest of the administration. In Pennsylvania, then-Governor Ridge gave the Office of Information Technology substantial authority to carry out its mission through both a management directive and an executive order that outlined his "priority to bring Pennsylvania to the forefront of the IT world." Interviewees in all states consistently cited support from top leadership as key to the success of the states' IT initiatives. As we explained earlier (S1.1), a direct reporting relationship to the governor's office can signal such support; but such structural arrangements do not by themselves guarantee that executive leaders will be effective champions of IT initiatives, as the California case illustrates.

S3.2. A Collaborative Management Style is a Key Factor in States with Exemplary IT Governance

A participative management style, with an emphasis on collaboration and communication, is important. There are two key aspects to this process. First, executive leaders involve staff in making decisions that affect them. Involving staff members helps create the buy-in that can make projects successful, which is particularly important in achieving organizational change. It also means that there are fewer surprises for personnel who are affected by changes in policies and procedures, which engenders trust in the leadership. (Note, however, that participative management should not be interpreted to mean that the CIO or governor gets too involved in or micromanages the day-to-day activities of his or her staff.) Second, teams are used to share information and make decisions. In the past decade, literature in management has stressed the value of using teams (e.g., Bikson, Cohen, & Mankin, 1998; Cohen & Bailey, 1997). In comparison to individuals, teams have a diversity of knowledge and skills to bring to their work, which enhances performance on complex tasks. Team collaboration enables organizational members to share information and perspectives that can improve local business processes. With respect to IT governance, collaboration gives staff opportunities to learn about other IT initiatives across the state and potentially join forces and realize greater economies of scale. A collaborative approach also provides opportunities for members of control agencies and client agencies to work together and develop the trust and interpersonal skills that support enterprise-wide efforts.

The primary role of business units or agencies in determining the goals of IT is emphasized in several empirical studies. A program to introduce IT in the Charlotte-Mecklenberg Police Department, for instance, began with several rounds of interviews and focus groups to find out what kind of information officers and other employees thought they needed in order to do their work better; once the resulting IT system was implemented, between half and three-quarters of officers perceived a three-fold or better improvement in performance, efficiency, call-response, and problem-solving productivity (Brown, 2001). Several studies emphasize the importance of letting business units or agencies who will use the IT set the agenda by proposing initiatives, controlling the financing, and being continuously involved in the planning and testing of IT projects (Radosevich, 2001; Internal Auditor, 1997; Kiely, 1997; Northrop, 2002; Avery, 2001). Two studies also demonstrate the benefits of using teams with diverse knowledge and skills; these researchers found that involving people with both business and technical expertise in procurement and outsourcing decisions was better than either group operating alone (Avery, 2001; Lacity & Willcocks, 1998).

In Pennsylvania, virtually everyone we interviewed identified the CIO's collaborative approach as a key factor underlying the success of IT. He meets regularly with agency CIOs and other agency IT personnel as well as with members of the OIT. He rarely issues mandates; instead, he involves personnel, uses a problem-solving approach to situations, and empowers staff to implement plans. For example, OIT's Bureau of Consolidated Computer Services (CCS), which was responsible for the consolidation of the Commonwealth's data center operation, had access to a large data center transition fund that could be used for unanticipated costs that arose during the consolidation effort. This allowed CCS to make quick decisions when faced with a roadblock, without having to go to the Office of Budget for each new request. A small amount of money is still available for this purpose, but it is used infrequently.

Consistent with a participative management style, the Pennsylvania CIO emphasizes "carrots" versus "sticks." One example of a carrot is funding to help agencies develop new IT projects. For instance, together with the Office of Budget, the CIO established a Technology Improvement Program, which provides seed money for agencies that develop cross-agency initiatives, particularly e-government applications. This money allows agencies to be responsive to rapid changes in IT without having to go through the 18-month funding and procurement cycle for each new purchase. OIT told agencies if they put together a business case outlining why their request was important and how they would partner with other agencies to show a single face of government, the money would be available to them to use.

The Pennsylvania CIO also is quick to give credit to agency personnel for IT successes; he makes an effort to recognize performance with rewards such as staff luncheons, T-shirts for transition leaders, and expressions of appreciation from himself or the governor by e-mail, videotape, or in person. Many interviewees described the CIO in terms such as "motivator," "team-builder," "creates an atmosphere of mutual respect," and so forth.

The Pennsylvania CIO uses collaborative approaches in other ways as well. He has a board of 18 corporate CIOs from the private sector (which excludes technology service providers to avoid conflicts of interest). As noted by an interviewee in Virginia, the states can learn a lot from the private sector, and credibility is enhanced when state decisionmakers have the backing of the corporate world. The Pennsylvania group meets quarterly with members of the OIT to provide advice and act as a sounding board. The CIO also collaborates with his peers in other agencies. For instance, he decided early on to form partnerships with his counterparts in the Office of Budget and Office of Human Resources, to keep them updated on the status of OIT's activities and involve them in decisionmaking. This effort has gone a long way in establishing trust in the CIO and OIT by the Office of Budget, which has financial authority over projects. It is unusual for Budget to reject a request supported by OIT because of this relationship. In addition, the former director from Budget now serves as the Chair of the Appropriations Committee in the state congress, a relationship that helps the OIT achieve its objectives via the legislature. The CIO's relationship with the Office of Human Resources has been advantageous as well because of its involvement with personnel and training issues.

Another important aspect of collaboration exemplified by the Pennsylvania CIO is his emphasis on building coalitions with local governments and explaining successful IT projects in terms of service delivery and benefits to local communities. For example, Pennsylvania's Justice Network (J-NET) is a nationally recognized model for interagency sharing of public safety information. OIT stressed successes like number of criminals taken off the street to illustrate the project's impact on the community. It also worked hard to get the endorsement of local police departments for the project. This grassroots support makes the selling of IT projects much easier, particularly to the legislature, which hears positive feedback from its constituents.

The Illinois Chief Technology Officer also exemplifies strong collaborative processes. The CTO lacks formal authority, so she relies mainly on communication and collaboration with state agencies to achieve IT objectives. Like the Pennsylvania CIO, she has a Board of Advisors comprised of agency CIOs. This board began as an informal complaint group, but now serves a formalized advisory role to the CTO. The CTO also serves as facilitator for a seminar series in which agencies present their IT activities to their peers. In addition, the CTO sponsors a popular exhibit hall at the state fair, called "Tech Town," where agencies present to the public how IT is used in government. The exhibit hall also serves as a networking and information sharing activity between agencies as they have the opportunity to learn about what each of the others is doing with IT in its organization. All of these activities facilitate important internal collaboration and information sharing.

The Secretary of Technology in Virginia too has an internal committee of agency CIOs and representatives of local government (the COTS board) as well as a CIO advisory board from the private sector (see http://www.cio.state.va.us/). However, several interviewees remarked that these resources could be used more frequently.

This does not mean that every decision is based on collaboration or that collaboration is always necessary for successful outcomes. For instance, in Pennsylvania, the previous governor mandated the decision to have a single email system and desktop software. This initiative, called "Commonwealth Connect," saved Pennsylvanians an estimated $9.2 million in software costs over three years and continues to save taxpayers an estimated $9 million a year in productivity gains and related savings, as calculated in a study conducted by Xerox. Standardization of email and desktop software also has facilitated communication and file sharing among employees. This initiative was a winner in the National Association of State Chief Information Officers 2001 Recognition Awards for Outstanding Achievement. In Virginia, the DMV was required to use VIPnet. As we described above, the DMV was successful in this initiative. Despite the compulsory nature of these projects, in both situations, the agencies affected by these decisions were given the freedom to determine how to implement the directives. This strategy is consistent with recommendations by Hackman (1998), who argues that teams are motivated to perform when they are given the ends (goals), but allowed to determine the means to achieve those ends. Of course, it is important to give goals that are achievable and to provide organizational resources and support that enable teams to meet their objectives (Hackman, 1998).

In the preceding discussion, we outlined and illustrated a number of success themes that characterize effective IT programs in states that rely on markedly different governance structures and processes. The next chapter treats IT governance challenges that all states must address and resolve—not necessarily in similar ways—to enable effective IT deployment.

5. Common Challenges to State IT Governance

Regardless of which approach to IT governance is taken, there are significant challenges to be addressed.

There are a variety of IT governance models for the State of California that could be made to work, given appropriate attention to the "success themes" mentioned in the previous chapter. But whichever approach is adopted, the resulting organization and staffing must address a set of "challenges," most of which involve making decisions about tradeoffs among competing interests and approaches. This process will often involve value judgments with no particularly right answers, but nevertheless these decisions will affect the way IT leadership, oversight, and management operate within California's government.

There are many such challenges. We have chosen to highlight the ones below because of the differing ways in which they have been handled in the states we studied, and our perception from interviews within California's departments and agencies that clear, consistent decisions and guidance about these challenges within California would help shape the state's IT policy. These challenges are ones that were mentioned by multiple respondents in our California and other state interviews.

We distinguish these challenges from the success themes listed in the previous chapter because these tend more toward value judgments for which there is no one right answer, but on which state government-wide consistency would be helpful in guiding the actions of individual department CIOs, agency information officers, and IT project leaders. We again describe these challenges within three topic areas: governance structure and organization of statewide functions; roles and functions of a statewide agency; and management style and context.

1. Governance Structure and Organization of Statewide Functions

Three challenges for a statewide IT agency involve the degree of centralization of IT functions to be attained; balancing outsourcing versus in-house development and operations; and handling state government-specific budget and turnover issues.

C1.1. Weigh the Advantages of Centralization Against Meeting Unique Agency Needs

There are many advantages of centralization of state IT functions. For example, such centralization would lead to greater standardization of software, in turn likely leading to savings in training, education, maintenance, and documentation. Centralized hardware (e.g., servers, switches, routers) can lead to less redundancy and more capacity; for instance, rather than each of several data centers providing its own spare capacity, it becomes more fungible and tradable within a central site. Centralized attention to information security is important, because this is becoming an ever more complex topic requiring specialized skills (e.g., in firewall configuration, intrusion detection systems, use of encryption schemes, and many other arcana). Yet, security is often only as good as the weakest link in the chain: one entry point into state systems through improper protection can provide access to others' systems and data. A centralized IT organization can also provide more of a career path for IT professionals than can smaller agencies within which IT is not a major business mission. For these and similar reasons, New York, for example, has plans to centralize into one state data center (with appropriate offsite redundancy), and to require use of only one set of office automation software, e-mail system, and the like throughout state operations.

And yet, agencies have unique requirements, differing relationships with their "customers" (state citizens and residents, businesses, and other constituencies), legacy information systems with differing hardware, software, interfaces, and so on. A policy of "one size fits all" can be inappropriate or costly.

Another factor must also be considered. When there are several distinct data centers or operations, new IT technology, ideas, or approaches can be considered and tested in one organization that might not be considered by other(s). In such a fast-changing field, such experimentation can be valuable to gain experience in solutions that are outside the prescribed standards.

There is a balance to be struck between centralization and decentralization, and that balance can vary depending on whether the focus is hardware, software, application programs and their development, networking, and so on. Policies and guidance in this general area will shape the state's IT plans and procedures, and should be given explicit attention by the state CIO and whatever IT management structure is put in place.

C1.2. Find a Balance Between Outsourcing and Developing In-House Competence

Some states, such as Pennsylvania and Illinois, have decided on considerable outsourcing of IT operations, including the operation of their data centers. Contractors are not subject to hiring freezes, wage levels, and other personnel constraints binding state governments. They can provide advantageous career paths, training and education, reward structures and the like for their staff. Through competitive bidding for such outsourced services, state governments may find savings over in-house operations. (For example, Pennsylvania has indicated that cost savings were achieved as a result of outsourcing, but did not give specific amounts.)

Yet such outsourcing of vital state IT operations and services can have significant disadvantages. IT skill levels may atrophy within government, making oversight and monitoring of outsourced operations more difficult. The state becomes highly dependent on a contractor that could become insolvent or bankrupt with little warning. State operations become tailored to the specific hardware and operating system configurations of that contractor, thereby becoming difficult to move or migrate to another contractor, or to bring back in-house.

These are complex tradeoffs for which statewide guidance and policies should be developed, especially if they involve the fundamental operations of a centralized state data center itself.

C1.3. Some Challenges Are Government-Specific

Large-scale IT projects are problematic in the best of circumstances. They often exceed budgets and schedules in the private sector, and the state government setting adds some factors making successful IT development even more challenging.[1] Two of them cited by interviewees in this study are: political forces influencing the continuity of the IT vision, and the lengthy state government budget cycle.

C1.3.1. Potential turnover of administrations every four years affects continuity of the statewide vision. An inherent challenge in operating in the public sector is the change in administration every four to eight years, and the resulting shift in the state's policy priorities and agenda. While many interviewees expressed the importance of executive-level support from the

---

[1]Interviewees in New York and Virginia mentioned examples of cost and schedule overruns, for example.

governor for IT, they also noted the negative effects of proximity to politics for the furtherance of IT goals. New executive leadership can bring changes to management and strategic direction, which may have been just implemented when a new entity takes over. This was cited as a serious challenge in Illinois, and particularly in Virginia because of the Commonwealth's law that no governor shall serve successive four-year terms. Interviewees noted that it usually takes a year for a new administration to become acclimated on the issues, leaving it with about two years to make progress on its agenda, before the last year when focus on the agenda begins to dissipate as the state looks forward to a new administration. Given the time needed to get new IT initiatives started because of long legislative, budget, and procurement processes, stakeholders may be reluctant to respond to new mandates, and simply "wait out" new initiatives pushed by an administration.

While this difficulty will always be present in the public sector, evidence from some states suggests that it is not impossible to make lasting progress toward IT goals. Collaborative initiatives that have gained buy-in from the key stakeholders in client agencies and from the legislature and that are tied to a strong strategic plan may be able to survive political shifts. For example, in Pennsylvania, interviewees said that the Commonwealth's data center consolidation and outsourcing effort cannot be threatened because it has shown how it is contributing to the global strategic plan for the Commonwealth, with proven successes recognized by the agencies. Further, modular projects also play a role in addressing this challenge. Well-designed modules can have value even if continued development is halted by an incoming administration. Large all-or-nothing initiatives, in contrast, will face major problems managing this challenge.

C1.3.2. A yearly budget cycle causes delays and constraints. A strong, recurring theme in our study's interviews was the negative effects of a rigid yearly government budget cycle on IT developments. This lengthy process almost guarantees that by the time a project receives funding, the assumptions built into feasibility studies regarding technology to be used, costs of hardware and software, and requirements to be met will have changed. In turn, these changes, when they exceed a modest threshold above or below the original estimate, will require generation of additional reporting and paperwork, such as filing of special budget requests or budget change proposals. These, too, enter into the yearly cycle and are in danger of obsolescence by the time they take effect. Another factor is that funding is on a yearly basis, increasing uncertainty that funds will be available in later years to complete a project that spans fiscal years.

Our study of other states provides some alternative strategies. In Illinois, agencies can be approved for multiyear appropriations up front, which frees

43

them from having to justify annual funding requests for approved projects from the Office of Budget.

New York, Pennsylvania, and Illinois each have a fund available to give agencies the opportunity to make certain kinds of IT purchases without having to go through the arduous 18-month budget cycle.

2. Roles and Functions of a Statewide IT Agency

We isolated five challenges related to the roles and functions of a statewide agency. Those challenges deal with procurement reporting requirements; IT versus a business strategy; developing metrics for measuring progress; creating an inventory of state IT equipment; and deciding on the appropriate degree of standardization.

C2.1. Determine What Amount of Arduous Procurement Reporting Requirements Is Needed for Accountability

Many California client agency personnel interviewed for this study would strongly prefer to be given a yearly IT procurement and operations budget to be used freely as they see fit, and then be judged on the results achieved. Instead, they spend very considerable time and resources preparing Feasibility Study Reports (FSRs), Special Project Reports (SPRs), and Budget Change Proposals (BCPs) to convince others (e.g., in the Department of Finance)—who know much less about their specific agency needs and operations—that what they wish to accomplish is reasonable, feasible, and manageable. There is some flexibility at the client agency level in how they spend an IT budget, but the project thresholds (in dollar amounts) above which these reporting mechanisms are to be used are very low given current costs.

These reporting mechanisms were put in place to provide both guidance and accountability at the state level, often because previous large-scale projects lacking such accountability were failures, or else ran considerably over budget or over scheduled completion time. Such mechanisms might also reflect a lack of trust.

With any new IT governance structure put in place, the balance between detailed reporting requirements for accountability and the levels of freedom of action provided to individual agencies should be reexamined. Part of this reexamination would involve study of *which* agency (e.g., Dept. of Finance, Office of the CIO) should review *which* reports and proposals (e.g., FSR, SPR, BCP), and with *what* level of authority to approve, veto, or otherwise control this accountability process. Those answers will also most probably depend on the amount of expenditure, over what period of time, that is contemplated for a new IT development or procurement. In any case, modular approaches to IT implementation should enable more efficient accountability and oversight processes.

C2.2. Determine Whether The Emphasis Should Be on an IT Strategy or a Business Strategy

Some interviewees questioned whether there should be an emphasis on a state IT strategic plan or agency IT plans. They argue that all IT developments should be justified by, and subsumed by, a business plan that concentrates on who the customer/recipient of the service is, how it might be provided, how this service fits in with larger agency plans and programs, and so on. IT is only a means to these ends, they say, and can only be understood within this larger context.

A side-effect of concentration on a business strategy is greater emphasis on departments and agencies as "business" units, rather than on a separate department of information technology, or a state IT strategic planning function. Even if a successor of DOIT is created in some form, California should balance the creation of IT-specific plans with agencies' desires for integrated business plans, of which IT is just a component.

C2.3. Determine the Proper Metrics for Measuring Progress in a Complex IT Development or Procurement

If a new agency is to be given an oversight role in major IT developments, what are the appropriate measures by which it can judge whether a development is on target or not? Clearly, simple measures such as expenditure of resources or lines of code produced are not sufficient. Any new oversight agency should give attention to articulating the metrics by which project developments are to be measured, and should discuss these measures with departments and agencies so that all parties know how oversight will be conducted.

We mention here a relevant "success theme" from the previous chapter: a strategy of modular development, starting with prototypes and then producing intermediate deliverables, so that the success of these intermediate waystations can be assessed. That strategy produces a set of metrics as a natural byproduct.

C2.4. Create a State IT Inventory and Ensure a Regular, Simple Refresh Cycle for Routine IT Office Equipment

In interviews with DOF and other IT control or client agencies, it was stated that in California there is no current overall inventory of state IT equipment. Unless a state knows what it has, it is hard to estimate what portion of that inventory will be coming up for replacement as part of a normal cycle during coming years. It is also more difficult to find redundancies or extra capacity that could be reallocated.

Interviewees also complained that normal, routine replacement of office automation equipment such as personal computers involved excessive justification and paperwork, rather than being treated as a normal, predictable process. Any revised IT oversight agency should consider means to regularize this process, including establishing guidelines for reasonable replacement intervals, so that it does not require needless delay or paperwork.

C2.5. Decide on the Most Appropriate Degree of Standardization

We have discussed the challenge of centralization of state IT resources above (C1.1). That is an issue regarding the structure of IT governance within the state. Distinct from that is the function of standardization, which we address here. A centralized IT agency may or may not impose a high degree of standardization, and decentralized IT agencies may decide to standardize on key hardware, software, or services (e.g., through use of a common General Services procurement agreement). There are both advantages and disadvantages to standardization, especially if carried to a high degree, which make decisions in this area challenging.

We were informed by the Office of the CIO in New York that it intends to standardize throughout the state government on one office automation package, one email system, and so on. It is unclear whether those plans will be carried through to that level of standardization, but there are clear advantages to be gained from it. For example, training, "help desk" functions, and software maintenance can be standardized throughout. It would also increase compatibility among diverse agencies in exchanging office documents, spreadsheets, database files, email, and the like.

However, such standardization might mean there is only one authorized supplier of office automation, or email, or database systems—raising questions of favoritism and locking out other suppliers. Once such standardization is

46

instituted, changing to other systems becomes difficult, requiring retraining of many thousands of government employees.

These decisions are perhaps even more difficult in California, with its Silicon Valley full of potential suppliers.

A decision facing any new IT governance in California is the appropriate degree of standardization of IT functions and systems throughout state government, weighing both benefits and disadvantages.

3. Management Style and Context

One management challenge we identified deals with the aging of the IT workforce in all of the states studied.

C3.1. Create an Approach for Handling the "Graying" of the State's IT Workforce

Most California interviewees mentioned the issue of the "graying" of the government's IT workforce, citing statistics showing the large number of baby boomers eligible for retirement. As this workforce cohort retires, who will maintain the legacy computer codes (e.g., written in COBOL) that operate many of the state's legacy business and service functions? Even if it were possible within the budget to hire replacement personnel, they are unlikely to have the needed skills or to want to learn these increasingly obsolete systems and programming languages.

This same problem is being encountered in other states, especially ones such as Illinois and New York that have "early out" retirement incentives for employees over age 55. Greater reliance on outsourcing of system operations is a possibility, but at the possible expense of a loss of some control. Understanding the magnitude of this problem across all government agencies and developing a strategy to handle it should be a priority for any new IT governance agency.

In this and the two preceding chapters, we have presented alternative structural models for effective IT governance, highlighting the success themes exemplified and the challenges that had to be resolved. The following chapter sets out the conclusions we draw and the recommendations we make for California's IT governance based on these findings.

6. Conclusions and Recommendations

We present here the key conclusions we believe can be drawn from this study and make recommendations regarding effective IT governance for California. Again, we structure both conclusions and recommendations within three categories: governance structure; roles and functions of a statewide IT agency; and management style. We trace our conclusions back to relevant success factors, challenges, and governance models, and point forward from those conclusions to relevant recommendations.

Conclusions

1. Governance Structure and Organization of Statewide IT Functions

Our survey of other states leads to the conclusion that:

N1.1. It is possible to provide visionary management, oversight, and control of major information technology initiatives at the state government level.

In other states, notably Pennsylvania and Virginia, we found effective governance mechanisms in place. To be sure, some projects had funding or schedule overruns. But we found capable management and frequent cooperation between IT/CIO leadership and budget/finance departments, resulting in an overall vision for service delivery and supporting infrastructure within the state, statewide IT projects vital to the states' operations, and improved ability to reach citizens and residents with needed services. Even central IT offices with a shorter history than the former DOIT had a longer track record of successful initiatives.

N1.2. There are several models of IT governance exhibited by various states; no one is the "right" one, but some are more relevant to California's current context than others.

In Chapter 3, we described three models of IT governance encountered in other states: "consolidated control," "collaborative leadership," and "advocacy." All three appear to be operating with considerable effectiveness within their own diverse state contexts. The models differ primarily in the degree of authority they give to a state-level IT office in technical, financial, operational, and procurement areas. It is possible to evolve from lesser to greater authority as a state-level IT office demonstrates competency and earns trust over time.

Regardless of governance model, the states we studied have an organizational statewide focus for IT developments. We conclude that California would be best served by reestablishing a state IT agency to act as that focal point (recommendation R1, below). Because of the size and scope of California's IT developments and procurements, and a poor track record to date for "collaborative" effectiveness in a California IT agency, we believe the "consolidated control" model may be appropriate for a new attempt at an effective California IT governance agency—while providing substantial in-house technical expertise in that agency to guide statewide development and procurement initiatives. Our recommendations, below, lead toward the establishment of an agency based on that model.

N1.3. Other states have decided that there are significant advantages in consolidating state data centers.

Almost uniformly, other state IT control and advisory agencies have concluded that there is considerable duplication and redundancy in their state's existing data centers, and that cost savings can be attained by consolidating them. A California interview noted that data centers offer duplicate services and that the economies of scale will not be realized until they are realigned along lines of services rather than the silo structures that now exist. Another state describes decreases in IT operating personnel from such consolidation of nearly 50 percent. Other reasons for consolidation are: (1) to create a career path for IT professionals that might not exist in individual client agencies; (2) to form a critical mass of expertise in IT skills and to promote uniform training of IT personnel in new techniques and technology; (3) to manage security of networks and nodes professionally and centrally, since any "weak link" in state information security might endanger other systems.

Deciding on the appropriate degree of centralization was listed as challenge C1.1. We find the reasons for greater centralization of IT services—and the need for that level of expertise in a new California IT agency—sufficiently compelling that we recommend (in R1.3, below) that California's data centers—particularly Teale—report to a single new IT agency.

N1.4. Direct support from the governor's office for critical statewide IT initiatives is a key success factor in other states.

In the four other states studied for this report, there is direct support for IT initiatives from the Office of the Governor. That support appears to be crucial in getting the diversity of agencies and departments "pulling together" toward a few common IT goals and systems needed statewide[1] (see success factor S3.1, above). California did not consistently receive such support for state-level IT initiatives.

The importance of this conclusion leads us to recommend (R1.1 and R1.2, below) that a new IT agency should report directly to the Office of the Governor, with the state's CIO possibly heading this new agency.

2. Roles and Functions of a Statewide IT Agency

Regarding appropriate roles and functions of a statewide IT agency, our primary conclusions are:

N2.1. Other state IT agencies conduct IT development activities and have been successful using a modular approach that provides both metrics for managing progress and tangible results to keep developers and clients motivated..

Modularity in IT development has two distinct aspects: (1) intermediate *deliverables*, allowing accomplishments to be measured, and (2) staged, incremental *deployment* of a system (e.g., by subsets of agencies).

The importance of modularity in IT system development and deployment was emphasized in success factor S2.2, above. The challenge of developing metrics is discussed in C2.3, above. This emphasis on modular development is reflected in recommendation R3.1, below.

N2.2. The yearly budget planning and approval cycle creates excessive delays and bureaucracy for major IT development/procurement initiatives.

Although development and approval of a yearly budget is a major control mechanism for California state government, it creates 18-month-long planning and approval rituals for major IT developments, which are often obsolete by the time funding and authority to proceed is received. Other states have used special funds as "incubators" for multiyear, multiagency IT developments to great effect, as a means of partially ameliorating the effects of the yearly budget cycle.

The unique characteristics of state government, and their effects on IT governance as well as IT budgets, were discussed as challenge C1.3. The

---

[1]An interviewee commented that California's response to Y2K exhibited all those positive characteristics: support from the highest levels of government, a clear goal, and success in marshaling resources throughout government to address the problem.

importance of having cross-fiscal-year "incubation" funds leads to our recommendation R2.4 regarding establishment of such funds in California.

3. Management Style and Context

We believe a focus on management style and context for statewide IT functions is important, because it recurs in discussions of "success factors" in other states, and as a reason for lack of success of the previous DOIT agency. Our conclusions in this topic area are:

N3.1. The former California DOIT was not sufficiently effective, for several specific reasons.

Several factors contributed to the lack of success of DOIT: (1) There appears to have been a lack of vision and prioritization of goals; DOIT attempted to do too much, spread too diversely, with its available resources. (2) DOIT was not given, in the end, the skilled, experienced personnel nor the clear authority (especially vis-a-vis roles of the Department of Finance) to accomplish what was needed. (3) A particular leadership style appears to be necessary (see following conclusion), and the previous management was not as effective as needed in this particular style of management.

This conclusion derives from the discussion of the former DOIT in Chapter 2, and the California interview summaries in Appendix B.

N3.2. Leadership style appears to be a critical success factor; genuine collaboration appears to be much more effective than hierarchical command-control.

A collaborative, cooperative management style appears to be a key "success theme" (see S3.2, above) in gaining the cooperation of client agencies, of the legislature, of budgetary/finance control agencies, and of the Office of the Governor. This management style is especially necessary in large state governments with competing interests, various control and client agencies (some with large constituencies and revenue sources), and differing branches of government.

We make an explicit recommendation regarding collaborative leadership style in R3.2, below.

N3.3. A variety of useful IT oversight/advisory mechanisms and partnerships are in use in other states. We discovered useful models of the composition and function of various advisory boards and other mechanisms for collaboration used to foster communication and cooperation among diverse agencies in other states.

There is also significant use of public/private partnerships as a means of providing expertise from companies to which some services and functions can be outsourced, without becoming dependent on them. These partnerships also either generate funds or save money for the state.

We recommend use of advisory boards for the new IT agency in R3.3, below.

N3.4. California's Department of General Services should be encouraged to utilize mechanisms that reduce the arduous processes for purchasing routine or standard equipment and services, such as master service agreements and statewide license agreements, while instituting safeguards to ensure fairness.

In other states studied, we found procurement of IT-related goods and services to be effective and efficient through the broad use of master contracts and agreements, with standard legal contract language promulgated for use by agencies, and with periodic outreach to, and solicitation of, new firms to be put under contract. Until recently, California also employed these types of agreements and licenses, but has since retreated from such mechanisms rendering most IT purchases subject to a lengthy procurement process.

N3.5. IT oversight and governance in California have now been reconsolidated within the Department of Finance; prior experience indicates that moving some of this power and control to a new agency will involve significant political infighting, possibly resulting in compromises that would again cripple the resulting new agency.

Lessons from the establishment of DOIT should be learned and mistakes not repeated. Under any foreseeable near-term future, Finance will retain overall budgetary control, as is appropriate. At present, it now asserts responsibility for "... providing oversight of the most critical IT projects ... and provide[s] direction, as necessary, on remediation efforts, ... and provide[s] appropriate notification to the administration and Legislature of project oversight activities, and project risks and remediation efforts."[2] That same document states that "... all IT policies and procedures will be promulgated through Finance [Budget Letters]." Any alternative agency or organization created to handle some or all such activities must necessarily wrest these powers from Finance, which will be reluctant—for understandable reasons—to see them placed in an untested,

---

[2]Budget Letter 02-37, "Statewide Information Technology Oversight," Department of Finance, October 16, 2002.

untrusted new agency. To the extent that the power to alter proposals for IT developments continues to rest within Finance, a number of interviewees (Appendix B) stated that a mechanism should be developed by which Finance is held accountable for delays, cost overruns, and other problems caused by such actions. At present, the burden and accountability for dealing with adverse effects of such Finance decisions appears to fall on the client agencies implementing these projects.

The following section states our recommendations for future IT governance in California, within the context of the above conclusions. Although opinions about the best path forward for California vary, we have tried to create a mutually consistent set of recommendations, compatible with our conclusions and having considerable explicitness, in order to provide a detailed structure and proposal for discussion. (In an earlier, interim briefing to key California IT professionals regarding our findings, such explicitness was requested by participants so that the implications of our recommendations could be debated and explored.)

Recommendations

There is a clear need for statewide IT system advocacy, planning, and coordination. These activities require a core cadre of professional IT specialists with significant skills. To achieve these goals, we make recommendations on (1) the structure and organization of a new IT agency for the state, (2) roles and functions to be performed by this agency, and (3) issues of management style and context for success.

1. Governance Structure and Organization of Statewide IT Functions

Based on our study's findings, we recommend that:

R1. A new agency of information technology should be established for California.

From the experiences of other states, showing the importance of the authority and interest of the Office of the Governor in creating momentum behind statewide IT initiatives, we recommend:

R1.1. This agency should report directly to the Office of the Governor.

It should be appropriate that the new agency be a cabinet-level office or otherwise have direct access to the Office of the Governor, to demonstrate the importance of IT developments within the state.

R1.2. The California Chief Information Officer (CIO) could remain as part of the governor's office (with the new agency reporting to it) or head this new IT agency.

To obtain and retain a critical mass of in-house IT expertise, and have responsibility and authority for statewide system security, we recommend that:

R1.3. Existing statewide IT data centers (e.g., Teale) should report directly to this new agency, and the new agency should have operational authority over statewide IT systems and services.

To the extent that the agency can demonstrate savings from consolidation, other agency data centers could, over time, become consolidated with the state data center.

R1.4. The existing offices of e-government and IT innovation, now located within the governor's office, should be consolidated within the new IT agency.

Among the activities these consolidated offices can perform—most likely in conjunction with advisory committees—is IT technology forecasting. These forecasts can help guide IT planning throughout the state's agencies and departments. To the extent that the e-government office has operational authority (e.g., operating the e-government portal for California), that authority should also reside in the new IT agency.

R1.5. The technical parts of the existing TIRU and TOSU groups within the Department of Finance should be transferred to the new IT agency. They should be responsible for reviewing major IT initiatives for consistency with the state IT strategy and priorities, with enterprise-wide applications (existing or planned), with technology standards, and with emerging trends (from forecasting). They will also review, initially and at follow-up intervals, proposed project management activities and progress metrics. The resulting recommendations should be reported to Finance, whose job will be to review the business case, taking into account the new IT agency's recommendations.

We recommend that not just the technology *charter* of these groups be transferred, but rather the majority of the *technical personnel* with the skills and experience existing within those groups should be transferred as well. With these skilled personnel and statewide data center personnel, the new IT agency will be properly staffed and positioned to provide technical approval and

54

oversight for major IT development projects. The suggested restructuring will have two effects. First, it seeds the key skills that the new governance organization will require to be successful. Second, it yields a clean division of responsibilities that minimizes overlap and competition.

It is important to underscore that operational responsibility and the experiences gained from it are central to the successful IT governance processes examined in this report. They provide the governance processes with two things. The first is credibility with agencies that are responsible for developing and operating IT systems—the governance process speaks from experience and becomes a peer with other agencies with responsibility for IT. The second is that experience tempers the IT strategy, recommendations (e.g., standards), and review processes—the governance is not seen as being theoretical but impractical in its findings and directions. Therefore, critical to the success of recommendation R1, above, are recommendations R1.3 and R1.5.

2. Roles and Functions of a Statewide IT Agency

We now consider roles and functions to be performed by the new IT agency.

R2. The key roles for the new IT agency involve advocacy of statewide IT initiatives, coordination of IT activities, and technical approval of major IT projects and procurements.

Among the specific activities that should be given priority by the new IT agency are these. (We list these in the approximate order in which they need to be addressed, either because of urgency or because some later activities depend on the results of earlier ones.)

R2.1. The new IT agency should be the "single voice" for advocating and developing statewide IT initiatives.

R2.2. The agency should develop and promulgate a statewide IT strategy and priorities for improving the performance of state missions.

R2.3. The agency should provide technology scanning and forecasting functions for the state and its agencies and departments.

R2.4. The agency should be provided a special fund to stimulate and promote new crosscutting IT initiatives. This fund should be replenished yearly, and not require normal budget review, allocation, and control procedures for its expenditures.

R2.5. The agency should stimulate development of significant crosscutting IT statewide applications, such as initiatives to enhance security of the state's information systems.

Information security and safety is one of the primary statewide IT initiatives that requires a high degree of technical skill and statewide coordination, since a "weakest link" in state IT systems may allow access to other agencies' data and systems.

R2.6. The agency should establish criteria (such as consistency with the state IT strategic plan, priorities, and metrics it develops for the effectiveness or importance of an IT initiative) by which new IT initiatives are to be judged and approved by Finance. Decisions on IT-related projects made by Finance should be justified by Finance in terms of these criteria, as well as in terms of the business case.

R2.7. The agency should lead in developing a statewide inventory of IT equipment and systems.

This inventory would serve as the baseline for understanding yearly costs for installed IT-related systems and services, and for establishing normal "refresh" cycles and their associated costs and savings for replacing outdated equipment.

3. Management Style and Context

Because of the importance of management style and context in successfully operating a state IT agency, we make several recommendations regarding management issues for the new agency:

R3. Establish a context and management style conducive to success.

The management approach of the new IT agency should rely on the success factors listed earlier in this report, and establish priorities for addressing the challenges listed. Several means for accomplishing this stand out:

R3.1. The agency should create an evolutionary strategy for IT developments stressing modular development and early successes and should involve stakeholders in planning and implementation.

Those early successes are vital in establishing trust for this new agency, upon which much of its effectiveness depends.

R3.2. The agency should develop regular, collegial relations among the new IT agency, the Department of Finance, the legislature, and agency and department CIOs.

Those relationships can include education (e.g., of legislators, regarding opportunities, costs, and benefits of new IT statewide initiatives), information sharing (e.g., regarding expected overall IT budgets for various departments and agencies within which those units' plans must be considered), and stimulation of shared IT initiatives among several departments or agencies that might allow sharing of development costs.

R3.3. The new IT agency and state CIO should be encouraged to establish advisory board(s) to help them assess future directions of IT technology and obtain lessons learned from IT governance within major corporations and nonprofit organizations.

These advisory boards should not, of course, have members with affiliations with organizations who are, or are potentially, suppliers of IT goods and services to the state.

R3.4. The agency should address "change management" issues, regarding how new systems, services, and capabilities are phased in and older ones phased out.

Particularly important in addressing change management is the treatment of state IT employees as new systems and skills are required, and older ones become obsolete. Effective (re-)training programs should be established, career paths for IT professionals developed, and issues of the "graying" of the workforce (with many workers due to retire in the coming years) addressed.

In summary, the proposed new IT agency has roles to play in all phases of the state's information technology development process.[3] For example,

- *planning*: developing a statewide IT strategic plan; technology forecasting; liaison with agencies' CIOs, Finance, and other participants in IT project planning
- *approval*: providing technical approval of major IT projects, or cross-agency and enterprise-wide projects; developing criteria by which such approval is judged

---

[3]This listing of development phases is taken from Figure 1 of "Information Technology: The State Needs to Improve the Leadership and Management of Its Information Technology Efforts," BSA, June 2001.

- *procurement*: providing periodic oversight of technical IT procurement processes, for example, to ensure a lack of conflict of interest

- *implementation*: developing and providing an IT project management skilled labor pool to assist other agencies as needed, and promoting modular, staged implementation of large-scale projects

- *evaluation*: developing metrics by which IT project success can be measured, consistent with the business plan within which they are operating.

We believe that the recommendations listed above are both feasible and important for the State of California. Through these measures, California can develop a vision and strategy for exemplary IT governance and can then deploy advancing technologies to achieve the state's key missions. In a period of resource constraints it is even more imperative that the power of information technology be focused on effective and efficient provision of services to the state's residents.

Appendix

A. State Profiles

New York

State size rank	3
Highest-level state IT office	Office of the New York State Chief Information Officer
Reporting structure	The Chief Information Officer reports to the Office of the Governor, but is not cabinet level. The Office for Technology (OFT), reports to the CIO as do other IT-related agencies, such as the Office for Cyber Security, that are not part of the IT office.
Advisory bodies	Two advisory bodies serve the CIO: the CIO Advisory Counsel comprised of agency CIOs who give feedback on proposed new technologies, and the Architecture Board representing stakeholders in enterprise-wide systems.
Technical authority	The OFT reviews agency IT project proposals and grants technical authority. The CIO is responsible for developing and enforcing IT policies and strategic plans. (Agencies must prepare strategic plans that are consistent with the state's plan and reflect its directions and priorities.) The CIO also decides on standards for basic platforms and enterprise-wide technology.
Operational authority	The IT office is responsible for the operation of the data centers as well as telecommunications and networks, including e-commerce. It is also responsible for training and mentoring client agencies in IT project management.
Procurement authority	The Office of General Services is responsible for most procurement, including smaller IT procurements following approval by the IT office. However, the IT office handles IT procurement when many or all agencies are involved. Additionally, the IT office reviews smaller IT procurement requests for consistency with planned or existing tools and platforms, and it approves all IT contractual agreements with vendors.
Financial authority	Financial authority rests with the Division of the Budget, which reviews the business case for IT projects and makes funding decisions. The state maintains a $10 million Technology Enterprise Fund from which the CIO and IT office can seed certain IT projects without going through the formal budget process.
Exemplary achievements	Won an award for its e-government web site, "Government without Walls."

Key Observations

Procedural

Project planning

- Agencies file Intent to Procure for each proposed project that is reviewed by the IT office; this is migrating to an Annual Technology Plan for each department or agency. Once implemented, all proposed projects will be included in the annual plan.
- The IT office created a "Project Management Guidebook"; client agencies contributed lessons learned to its development.

Approval (technical and budget)

- The IT office places projects in three categories: (1) strategic; (2) continuing expenditure; (3) attrite/retire. OFT decides whether it will grant technical approval based on the status of a project in one of these three categories.
- "Agency budgets tend to dominate in normal times." Generally, agencies must work with the Office of Budget to receive IT project funding. For special initiatives such as Y2K preparation, however, agencies received allocated funds from OFT.

Procurement

- The Office of General Services has many products covered by standing contracts, which can be ordered directly. For example, standing contracts cover 20 different brands of personal computers. Services/technology can also be obtained on broad, existing contracts. These standing contracts have standard "boilerplate" terms and conditions, which, if used, speed the procurement process.
- There is a "mini-bid" process; vendors are preapproved (up to about $250,000) for consulting services. This greatly speeds procurement of such services.

Project oversight

- Project oversight is primarily the responsibility of client organizations, except when interagency coordination is needed by the Office of the Chief Information Officer.

Management

Enterprise-wide governance across state agencies

- The new CIO has plans to consolidate three data centers into one (with backup; there were 25). He plans to standardize much of the office automation software, e-mail, personnel software, etc.
- The state has a "Technology Entrepreneurial Fund," with about $10 million that the IT office can allocate to some projects, and roll over funding to subsequent years.

Strategic planning

- The state is using Ohio's five-page IT strategic plan as a template; individual agency strategic plans will be required to be much more detailed, and will be reviewed by the CIO's office for consistency with the statewide strategic plan prepared by the IT office.

Leadership style

- Consolidated Control. The CIO believes he has authority from the governor to act boldly in creating standards, centralization, and consistency across agencies and departments, and eliminating waste and redundancy. Client agencies argue, "one size fits all isn't going to work."

Workforce issues

- New York lost many state employees age 55 and older from an "early retirement initiative" program.
- Agencies complain they can't compete for IT skills.

Technology

Infrastructure development

- The IT office has an annual budget of about $250 million. Most of the budget is for data center and telecommunication services provided to other agencies and billed to the agencies. About $50 million a year is internal to the IT office.

Standards, technology forecasting

- The state is organizing an "Architectural Board," which will serve as an advisory board to the CIO council on standardization issues.

- The "Project Board" is involved in large project management.

Illinois

State size rank	5
Highest-level state IT office	Illinois Technology Office
Reporting structure	Chief Technology Officer (CTO) sits within the governor's office and reports to him directly.
Advisory bodies	The Chief Technology Officer is served by an advisory body of agency CIOs.
Technical authority	Client agencies develop IT project proposals with input and guidance from the CTO, but projects receive approval from the Strategic Planning Office and Office of Performance Review in the Bureau of Budget. Project evaluation is carried out by the Office of Performance Review.
Operational authority	Operational authority for data center services are mostly decentralized; agencies manage (almost) all operations, many of which are outsourced.
Procurement authority	Central Management Services (CMS) has authority for all procurement. Although the CTO has no authority for procurement, it is working with CMS in its effort to establish standards that have major implications for procurement.
Financial authority	The Bureau of Budget has authority for all funding requests.
Exemplary achievements	• Received "Digital State" award in 2001 for use of technology in government • In the few years since its creation, it has managed to establish 22 state-level IT projects

Key Observations

Procedural

Project planning

- Projects are initiated by agencies, with guidance from the CTO.

Approval (technical and budget)

- Some projects are approved for multiyear appropriations up front so agencies do not have to request funds repeatedly.

Procurement

- Central Management Services established master contracts with vendors that reduce the time and effort required by agencies to purchase hardware and software.

Project oversight

- The Performance Review Office uses the Illinois Technology Enterprise Planning System (ITEPS), a software system used to measure progress on projects by tracking agency IT plans and requests; performs project oversight.

Management

Enterprise-wide governance across state agencies

- The CTO has a Special Information Technology (SIT) Project Fund, which is used to fund IT projects proposed by agencies that make a compelling business case for the improvement of customer service or increased efficiency or economy for the state. The Office of the Chief Technology Officer reviews the proposals, ranks the projects by priority, and approves the funding. The central fund was appropriated $26 million in 1999 as a revolving fund, which means that it does not have to be reappropriated each year. The funds have been used for a variety of projects. According to the Illinois CTO, the money has been very useful in jumpstarting new initiatives, such as in the area of e-government where the money is combined with other sources of funds. The CTO's office reports quarterly on the status of the fund and projects to the Bureau of Budget, Central Management Services, the agencies, and the Executive Office of the Governor.
- The CTO facilitates communication and collaboration among state agencies by:
  — formally involving agency CIOs through an advisory board that meets regularly;
  — hosting an internal seminar series for agencies to share IT activities with each other; and,
  — sponsoring "Tech Town," an exhibit hall at the annual state fair where agencies present to the public how they are using IT to deliver services.

64

Strategic planning

- Agencies are required to address IT in their strategic business plans; the Strategic Planning Office integrates these plans into the statewide plan within the Bureau of Budget (a cabinet-level department).

Leadership style

- Advocacy. The CTO has no formal authority, but has made progress by brokering strong relationships with the budget and procurement departments, the agencies and the Legislature.
- The placement of the Technology Office within the governor's office gives the CTO access to executive support and the ability to influence in the absence of formal power; the disadvantage of the arrangement is the greater susceptibility of political entanglements.

Workforce issues

- The state is losing many employees age 55 and over because of the Early Retirement Initiative (ERI); critical knowledge about legacy systems will be lost and ability to hire replacements is in question.
- Some look at the ERI as an opportunity to boost innovation in state government.

Technology

Infrastructure development

- Bids were due in November 2002 on a CTO-developed RFP for centrally funded Public Key Infrastructure initiative for use by state agencies. The purpose of this initiative is to establish an enterprise-wide infrastructure for facilitating government services by verifying the identity of users and the authenticity of documents.
- Illinois achieved de facto standardization through the use of a master contract for the purchase of Geographic Information System (GIS).
- The CTO established web accessibility standards for agency websites.

Standards, technology forecasting

- Master contracts create de facto standards by providing an incentive for agencies to use standard terms and conditions with selected vendors.

- The Technology Office is tasked with identifying appropriate standards for the state, but has encountered difficulty because of procurement concerns about fairness.

Pennsylvania

State size rank	6
Highest-level state IT office	Office for Information Technology (OIT)
Reporting structure	The CIO, as a Deputy Secretary, reports to the cabinet-level Office of Administration Secretary. The OIT, comprised of seven organizational units, reports to the CIO.
Advisory bodies	The CIO has a advisory body comprised of 18 private-sector CIOs that provide guidance on enterprise-wide projects.
Technical authority	The Office for Information Technology reviews and approves agency project plans and makes recommendations to the Office of Budget for funding. OIT sets the guiding vision for IT in the state and develops standards for IT products and procedures with substantial feedback from agencies.
Operational authority	OIT has operational authority over data centers and basic computer and network infrastructure as well as enterprise-wide initiatives.
Procurement authority	The cabinet-level Department of General Services (DGS) is responsible for statewide policies and procedures for procurement. Hardware procurement is managed by DGS, which maintains a list of prequalified vendors. Small acquisitions are done by agencies themselves from those vendors; large acquisitions are handled by DGS via bidding to achieve economies of scale. DGS delegates routine procurement of IT services to OIT, which developed a master services contract and method for pre-qualifying vendors. Large software and system integration procurements are also delegated to OIT; DGS helps guide and review the bids and contracts.
Financial authority	The Office of Budget has financial authority for IT projects. Although OIT formally has an "advisory role" to OB, in practice "the Budget Office usually concurs."
Exemplary achievements	- Received the National Association of State Chief Information Officers 2001 Recognition Awards for Outstanding Achievement for the Commonwealth's e-mail and software standardization effort, "Commonwealth Connect" - Received "Best of Breed" award from the Center for Digital Government for e-government portal in 2002 Successfully consolidated data centers from 23 to 1 - Standardized e-mail and desktop applications statewide - Technology Investment Program

Key Observations

Procedural

Project planning

- IT initiatives for agency-specific applications are planned and managed by agencies but comply with policy planning guides (from OB) and IT standards (from OIT/OA). Concept plans and draft budgets are submitted early for feedback, with detailed plans and budgets to follow.

- Enterprise-wide initiatives may be generated by OIT or bottom up—when multiple agencies submit concept plans reflecting shared needs. OIT is responsible for enterprise-wide projects, with formal guidance from agency representative.

Project oversight

- Agency-specific initiatives are overseen by the agencies; methods vary.

- Large or enterprise-level projects require quality assurance by the IT provider, with oversight from an advisory body of agency representatives (may use measurable milestones or benchmark against other states); a consulting firm may do an independent review.

Management

Enterprise-wide governance across state agencies ("Breaking Through Barriers," a 1996 strategic plan, announced this aim)

- OIT led consolidation of data centers from 23 to 1; it outsources center operations but retains oversight and management.

- OIT standardized desktop technologies and implemented a common, centralized email system; this saves over $9 million a year in technology costs (not including savings on maintenance, support, training, and integration).

- OIT has "Technology Investment Program" (TIP) money—seed funds for investing to "kick start" agency initiatives, especially ones that may diffuse beyond the originating agency. $20–30 million is set aside annually by the Office of the Budget and the legislature for the program. OIT gives the legislature a list of types of projects it thinks will be covered by the funds, but it is given significant flexibility to move the funds around as it sees fit.

Strategic planning

- While "Breaking Through Barriers" is still a guiding vision, Pennsylvania no longer requires annual strategic plans (invariably will need mid-course corrections). Now OIT develops brief guiding principles and direction-setting objectives.

- Individual agencies vary in approaches: some do regularly updated IT strategic plans; others argue that strategic plans should focus on mission performance (no need for an IT strategic plan separate from the business strategy).

Leadership style

- Collaborative, participatory. Agency CIOs have "dotted line" relationships to state CIO, who meets quarterly with them and also encourages informal communication ("open door" policy). Enterprise projects have agency representatives on advisory boards with formal voting rights. State CIO "really empowers" agency CIOs, maintains strong collegial ties to counterparts in OB and DGS.

Workforce issues

- Concern over civil service hiring and salary constraints (can't compete with private sector for IT talent).

- "The graying of the mainframers" will create problems for maintaining big systems.

- Outsourcing of back-end system operations works well, with OIT performing highly skilled oversight. With consulting advice from KPMG, OA/OIT decided to consolidate its data centers and outsource the operational functions but to keep applications development and ownership in the agencies. OA/OIT, however, continues to act as the permanent oversight organization. "Back-end" functions include mainframe upgrades, both in hardware, software, and services; data processing and hosting of data processing systems; and backup and security.

Technology

Infrastructure development

- Centralized funding for enterprise-wide projects to accommodate needs of small and large agencies (plus "incubator" TIP).

- Strong push toward modular development (e.g., enterprise resource planning modules) and incremental implementation (deploy in selected subsets of agencies over time) to yield steadily growing functionality and promote "positive change orientation, fed by small successes" visible in relatively short periods. The Enterprise Resource Planning (ERP) software that Pennsylvania has chosen (SAP) can, like most ERP systems, be implemented and used in relatively self-contained but subsequently integratable parts (for instance, the financial accounting package might be implemented first, then the payroll system, and so on).

Standards, technology forecasting

- Standards (procedural, product-oriented, or hybrids) are circulated in draft Information Technology Bulletins (ITB) by OIT for response before finalization; agency comments can affect the final standard. Standardization is generally welcomed now.

- Agencies track IT developments in mission-specific areas by participation in professional societies, use of consulting groups, and benchmarking against counterparts in other states. OIT is charged with promoting IT innovation; a council of private sector CIOs reviews and comments on proposed new initiatives.

Virginia

State size rank	12
Highest-level state IT office	Secretariat of Technology
Reporting structure	The Secretary of Technology is part of the cabinet and reports to the governor. The Secretariat of Technology consists of four agencies, headed by the Secretary, which include the Department of Technology Planning (DTP), the Department of Information Technology (DIT), the Center for Innovative Technology, and the Virginia Information Providers Network Authority.
Advisory bodies	Council on Technology Services (COTS) board consists of CIOs of some state agencies and members of local government, and advises the Secretary of Technology. Advice tends to be conceptual rather tactical. Some members don't participate on a regular basis; they argue that the COTS board is not as involved as it could be. CIO advisory board is comprised of CIOs in the private sector and meets infrequently.
Technical authority	For projects over $100,000 but less than $1 million, the Secretary of Technology or his designate (usually the Department of Technology Planning) has project approval authority. For projects over $1 million, the Secretary of Technology must give approval. The Secretary of Technology has veto power. The Department of Technology Planning sets guidelines for IT development, which are voluntary, as well as standards, which are required for agencies to follow.
Operational authority	The Department of Information Technology (DIT) runs the data centers and telecommunications.
Procurement authority	The Acquisition Services Department in the Department of Information Technology has procurement authority for IT purchases.
Financial authority	The Department of Planning and Budget has financial authority for IT projects.
Exemplary achievements	• Received "Best of Breed" award from the Center for Digital Government for e-government portal in 2002 • Innovative public/private partnership for IT projects

Key Observations

Procedural

Project planning

- Projects are initiated by agencies and submitted to DTP annually.
- DTP handles enterprise-wide strategic planning.

Procurement

- Previously, agencies handled their own procurement with the Department of General Services. On July 1, 2002, a new law was passed that delegated all of IT procurement to the Acquisition Services Division in the Department of Information Technology.

Project oversight

- Project oversight is largely decentralized. For large projects, DTP has oversight responsibility, but it has been inconsistent. In some cases, DTP was involved from the beginning of project; in others, it was not involved until the project was in trouble.

Management

Enterprise-wide governance across state agencies

- Agencies are responsible for their own equipment and applications. They have access to DIT services, but large agencies often have in-house expertise. Currently, project governance is highly decentralized.

Strategic planning

- Strategic planning is currently decentralized. Some agencies do regularly updated IT strategic plans; others argue that IT should support the business plan.
- The Secretary of Technology recently announced a sweeping IT strategic plan to centralize all IT resources, systems, and control; it is described as the most ambitious in the country. It will eliminate DIT and DTP and integrate them with IT personnel and resources from all agencies (this will involve consolidating 2300 personnel) into a new IT control agency.

Leadership style

- Centralized control. The Secretary of Technology has designed an extensive strategic plan with little input from agency heads and CIOs. His office is drafting legislation to gain increased control over IT policy. Agency IT personnel are concerned about the "one size fits all" plan.

Workforce issues

- There are some concerns about the graying of the IT workforce, particularly for legacy systems.

Technology

Infrastructure development

- Agencies are responsible for implementation.
- Secretary of Technology's office is considering a plan for an enterprise-wide fund to assist agencies.

Standards

- DTP develops guidelines and standards. Guidelines are voluntary, unless an agency is rated obsolescent in an IT area. Standards are required, and agencies must determine how to implement them.

B. California Interview Summaries

Organizations Interviewed

Control Agencies and Departments

- Current CIO
- Department of Finance
- Department of General Services

Client Agencies and Departments

- Franchise Tax Board
- Employment Development Department
- Board of Equalization
- Youth and Adult Correctional Agency
- Business, Transportation and Housing
- Department of Transportation
- Department of Motor Vehicles
- Health and Human Services Agency

Technical Agencies

- Teale Data Center
- Health and Human Services Data Center

The following is a listing of key comments received during our interviews within the above California departments and agencies. They represent a range of opinions offered by interviewees. We have mainly included comments that had support from more than one interviewee, but they cannot, of course, be considered as statistically representative of the opinions of IT-relevant personnel across all of California governmental agencies.

Procedural

Project Planning

- Some agencies/departments are relatively mature with respect to internal governance processes; they employ a series of procedures to judge and assess IT projects before an FSR is submitted. This helps to ensure that the proposals are better.

- Executives must be knowledgeable and proficient in the role and decision process for IT. Previous formalized attempts did not last.

- IT is supported at the high levels of government: there is awareness and support, but there is some misunderstanding of the topic of IT and what it takes to implement it.

- Up-front coordination (pre-FSR delivery) between control and client is considered a useful step to mitigate surprises once the FSR is delivered. This process has seen limited use and limited success. Clients are concerned that DOF will not have an appreciation for the project if they are not involved in the conceptual development, while DOF is concerned about compromising its authority.

- FSRs are done with extreme detail and care as they determine funding approval and project baseline. However, at this point the project is in the early definition stage and there may be undue confidence in the accuracy of these details (by control organizations).

Approval (technical and budget)

- There was significant ambiguity of DOIT's role and responsibilities relative to other control organizations for approval. This eroded trust and confidence in them from the agency/department perspective.

- The approval process appears to client organizations at times preferential, arbitrary and unilateral. Control, however, identifies key questions that guide approval. A statewide entity could work with DOF to direct which things should be funded.

- Accountability for project performance is not perceived as commensurate with authority for approval, funding, and oversight by client organizations. However, control organizations indicate that under DOIT, department directors had responsibility for project success, unlike its predecessor OIT, where there was confusion about responsibility.

- Departments and agencies are frustrated with the additional time the approval and budgeting process adds to getting a project initiated.

- The challenges associated with the control processes motivate behaviors to avoid the control process.

- A statewide entity could include roles related to approval and budgeting that balance the fiscal project assessment perspective.

Procurement

- Departments/agencies are exploring nontraditional procurement strategies that leverage industry knowledge and resources (business based, performance based). However, these efforts have not been widely embraced due to challenges associated with funding and procurement.

- The tension between enterprise efforts for cost efficiency and effectiveness and competitive procurements for equity and public trust makes it difficult for the state to leverage its buying power.

- The state must provide training programs for procurement vehicles so departments understand the intent of each one. Departments didn't understand the intent of CMAS and they started using it for IV&V and other ongoing work. These efforts were intended to reduce procurement time and minimize redundant purchasing actions.

Project Oversight

- Project oversight occurs at many levels internal and external to departments/agencies, but there are varied opinions on how much is necessary and where it should occur. DOF is currently revising the oversight structure to allow a hierarchical, graduated process.

- As a result of highly publicized failures with political implications, the oversight process has evolved and expanded with the objective of preventing the next fiasco. However, a broader oversight definition includes both a control and collaborative perspective.

- "Failed IT" as a label may be overused, because the definition of failure (variance to budget or schedule) is too narrow.

Management

Enterprise-Wide Governance Across State Agencies

- California needs an enterprise-wide structure for IT; the federated nature of the state will make that difficult. Policy needs to accommodate the diversity of agencies and departments.

- A statewide entity could provide a forum for the IT community to address many of the common issues, such as sharing data, common (redundant) applications, and a project repository (method to identify like objectives) for leverage.

- A statewide entity could provide strategic thinking from an enterprise perspective. Leverage the departments collectively for buying power and statewide systems evolution. (See also Procedural—Procurement)

- A statewide entity could communicate the challenges and benefits of IT.

- A statewide entity could be responsible for centralized functions that are ubiquitous, that touch all aspects of government rather than one that analyzes the details of projects. If not, the ability to see the bigger perspective is lost. It is going to be essential to have a centralized or statewide entity that could speak to, fund, advance, advocate, and vet some of the initiatives that are in interest of the state as whole.
  — Centralize the security function.
  — Centralize the evaluation of advanced technology products. Departments are duplicating efforts. There should be pilot efforts to test new technology that could be used by multiple departments.
  — Centralize the project management function.

- The promise of enterprise IT governance may benefit from agency reorganization, which offers opportunities for efficiencies.

Strategic Planning

- IT strategic planning must be done in concert with business planning, based on the mission.

- Statewide strategic planning is challenging because California is a huge conglomerate, no single authority for all agencies/departments, no pool of funding to support it.

- The strategic plan should have broad stakeholder involvement with objectives for improving California and how IT supports that goal.

- A statewide entity could centralize and establish the statewide IT direction (strategy) and policy.

Leadership

- DOIT was not recognized as a leader (ineffective coordination of statewide strategic plan, limited utility of agency/department information management plans and activity reports, inconsistent responses to inquiries, staff turnover and limited agency/department knowledge, standards development wasn't responsive to department/agencies).

- Three incarnations of IT governance (SOIT, OIT, DOIT) all had similar constructs and all faced with similar challenges—achieving collaboration.

- Leadership challenges for DOIT included perceptions of ineffectiveness, political turf battles, and limited authority.

- A statewide entity that does policy and vision should be separate from project approval and oversight.

- A statewide entity must be knowledgeable, have integrity and the authority for the "voice" of IT to include recommending where California should direct funding, minimizing approval time and look at enterprise-wide issues such as departments going it alone, with others, or via data centers.

Workforce

- Outsourcing and training are strategies to compensate for unique skills, aging skill base, and workforce shortages.

- The state is unable to compete for IT staff (industry, on-line testing, job classifications).

- The state's system for personnel is major challenge (person years allocation).

- A statewide entity could address delivering services when the systems we depend on are losing people.

Technology

Infrastructure Development

- Agencies/departments develop their own systems when a central organization cannot meet their critical need, but data centers could be used to provide common needs, economies of scale, and security.

- A statewide entity could include the data centers.

Standards, Technology Forecasting

- Standards are needed, but this is politically problematic.

C. A Summary of the Department's Progress

The Bureau of State Audits made a variety of recommendations to the Department of Information Technology (DOIT) in its June 2001 report. The table shows the bureau's recommendations and DOIT's progress in implementing those recommendations as of its sunset date of July 1, 2002.

Recommendations	DOIT's Progress
To provide strategic guidance for the State's IT activities, DOIT, in conjunction with the departments, the governor, the Legislature, the Department of Finance, and other relevant parties, needs to update the statewide IT plan to address the current IT environment. In particular, the plan should establish measurable objectives to show how the State intends to reach its goals. Also, the plan should communicate priorities for approval and funding of projects. To facilitate the establishing of such priorities, DOIT should work in collaboration with the entities previously mentioned.	Not fully implemented. DOIT drafted a statewide IT plan. However, DOIT management stated that this plan was still incomplete.
To ensure departments' IT strategic plans are consistently evaluated for their compliance with the statewide IT strategy, DOIT should implement a process to review department plans.	Not fully implemented. DOIT made some progress in developing a way to review departments' IT strategic plans through the use of an enhanced strategic plan review checklist. However, after developing this enhanced checklist, DOIT granted the departments until August 2002 to bring their strategic plans into compliance. Since the August 2002 deadline was after DOIT's sunset date, this checklist was never used.

Recommendations	DOIT's Progress
To provide appropriate department guidance and direction for the IT development process, DOIT should consolidate the various sources of policy and guidance, remove outdated policies from published documents, and revise policies as needed to reflect changing state needs. In addition, DOIT should resolve the contradiction between its management memorandum and the State Administrative Manual over the applicability of the alternative procurement process. Finally, DOIT should work with General Services to evaluate the alternative procurement process and provide information to departments about how the process could be most effectively used.	Not fully implemented. DOIT developed a framework to manage its policies, procedures, and guidelines to update its guidance issued to state departments. The framework defined whether such documents would be maintained in the State Administrative Manual or the Statewide Information Management Manual. In addition, DOIT stated that it had reviewed IT policies, procedures, and guidelines and provided recommendations to consolidate or remove specific outdated documents. However, DOIT did not implement these recommendations. DOIT rescinded the management memorandum that conflicted with the State Administrative Manual and deferred all future policy decisions regarding the alternative procurement process to General Services.
DOIT should continue its efforts to improve its project review and approval process. However, it should ensure that the changes result in a process that will subject proposed IT projects to a thorough evaluation. Further, DOIT should ensure that departments are properly assessing IT projects by comparing departments' feasibility study reports with established criteria, such as the fundamental decision criteria. Moreover, to ensure that it can defend its approval of costly IT projects, DOIT should thoroughly document its approval decisions.	Not fully implemented. DOIT did not ensure it fully documented its project review decisions. In all twelve of the projects we reviewed, DOIT could not provide evidence that it tracked the departments' compliance with the conditions it included in the project approval letters DOIT sent notifying them of its concerns.
To ensure departments assess and mitigate project risks, DOIT should require complete risk assessment reports from departments. Further, DOIT should properly analyze the responses and document how it resolves any concerns. Finally, DOIT should require departments using the alternative procurement process to assess risks at the beginning of their projects. If DOIT believes its current model is inappropriate for alternative procurements, it should modify its risk model to more appropriately address alternative procurements.	Not fully implemented. DOIT stated that it had enhanced the Risk Assessment Model (RAM) and ensured that it applied to all projects, regardless of the procurement process. However, DOIT could not provide consistent evidence that it reviewed the RAMs the departments submitted. In addition, we could not see a strong linkage between the risk-related comments submitted by the departments in their RAMs and the risk-related comments made by DOIT for those RAMs it reviewed.

Recommendations	DOIT's Progress
To ensure that it receives and effectively uses the proper information to monitor departments' IT projects, DOIT should take the following actions: • Continue with its efforts to restructure the oversight process to ensure that the process allows DOIT to properly monitor and guide projects. • Modify the required progress reports to include two types of critical information: the project's monthly actual costs and revised estimates of total projected costs compared with the budget, and actual and revised projected completion dates for project phases compared with the original schedule. DOIT should use this modified progress reporting to closely monitor projects that may be required to submit special project reports. • Ensure that analysts sufficiently review and document their oversight of projects and track the receipt of required reports.	Implemented. DOIT modified its project status report to include approved budget, budget variance, expenditures to date, and planned and actual start and completion dates for major project milestones. DOIT adequately accounted for these reports. DOIT also modified the project approval letter that required certain conditions be met.
To hold departments accountable for the benefits expected from their IT projects, DOIT should ensure that departments submit post implementation evaluation reports (PIER). Further, DOIT should continue with its effort to reengineer the evaluation process including the incorporation of lessons learned from project development.	Not implemented. DOIT management stated that they did not track projects for the purpose of ensuring that departments submitted their PIER documents.
To promote coordination on IT projects and avoid redundant efforts, DOIT should establish a formal mechanism to initiate discussions between departments that are developing projects based on similar technologies or processes. To facilitate this coordination and improve project oversight, DOIT should complete its IT project inventory based on its survey of departments. DOIT should ensure that departments' reported data are accurate and should update this information when departments report new information so that the project inventory stays current. DOIT also needs to consider how departments and the Legislature can effectively access this information, taking into consideration privacy issues and other concerns that may limit the release of this information.	Not fully implemented. To fulfill this recommendation DOIT facilitated meetings with two groups. The first was the Information Technology Coordination Council/Enterprise Coordination Council (ITCC/ECC), which consisted of Agency Information Officers and Chief Information Officers (CIO) Workgroup chairpersons. The second was the CIO meetings. The primary items discussed in these meetings focused on policy decisions. More specifically, according to the meeting notes, DOIT seemed to be using these meetings to get input on developing IT standards and policies. While this was a valuable activity, our recommendation specifically calls for a formal mechanism to initiate discussion between departments that are developing projects based on similar technologies or processes. In addition, DOIT did not complete its IT project inventory. Although DOIT conducted a survey of departments, at the time of its sunset none of this information had been reviewed for accuracy or completeness.

Recommendations	DOIT's Progress
To improve compatibility and properly guide IT development, DOIT should expedite its work on implementing standards by determining which standards need to be addressed first and focusing their efforts accordingly. Further, DOIT should work with departments to ensure that all necessary standards have been implemented.	Not fully implemented. As of its July 1, 2002 sunset date, DOIT had not developed and issued standards for security, infrastructure, accessibility, data or applications development. Rather, DOIT issued general policies for three of the five categories it identified—security, infrastructure, and accessibility. These policies offered general objectives but did not provide the standards that are needed to ensure consistency, compatibility, and effectiveness among departments.
To ensure that DOIT is fully employing the IT advisory councils and receiving the benefits intended by law, DOIT should continue to meet with the private commission and the public committee on a regular basis to guide its strategic planning efforts, provide input on new policies, and ensure that the State follows best practices. DOIT should ensure that the public committee makes all findings and recommendations in writing, as required by state law. DOIT should also monitor the progress of its CIO work groups to ensure that they reach their established goals.	Implemented. To fulfill this recommendation DOIT met with three groups: the ITCC/ECC, CIO, and the California Information Technology Commission (CITC). Based on our review of DOIT's agendas and notes from those meetings, we found that DOIT met with these groups (the ITCC/ECC and CIO groups served as the public committees while the CITC served as the private commission) on a regular basis to receive guidance for its strategic planning efforts, to receive input on new policies, and to discuss best practices issues.
To ensure that it completes initiatives, DOIT should establish timelines and goals for meeting future initiatives. If DOIT does not believe it can complete initiatives within established guidelines, it should communicate its priorities and resource requirements to the Legislature. In addition, it should notify the Legislature when a change in the State's IT environment prompt adjustments to these priorities or resource requirements.	Not implemented. DOIT management stated that, as of its July 1, 2002 sunset date, it would cease operations. In order to protect the State's $1.7 billion IT portfolio, DOIT stated that the administration was committed to establishing a short-term interim IT oversight agency. This interim agency will continue to assess how to reorganize the operation and management of California's IT systems after July 1, 2002, and will continue to communicate with the Legislature regarding changes in the IT environment that require adjustments to priorities and resources.
To organize and focus its efforts, DOIT should adopt an internal strategic plan to identify key responsibilities and establish priorities. This plan should clearly describe how the organization would address its many responsibilities, particularly those that we observed it has not sufficiently accomplished. Further, it should build on past efforts to the extent possible rather than reinventing processes and practices when planning its future activities.	Not fully implemented. DOIT management stated that it completed much of this recommendation with the publication of its 2001–2004 Strategic Plan, but did not complete its business plan as part of that effort before its sunset date.

D. Literature Review

In our literature search, we used the following databases and keywords.

Databases

ECO, EconLit, Wilson Business Periodicals, Social Science Abstracts, Business Management Practices, PAIS, ERIC

Search Strategy

In Subject/Descriptor field: Information Systems Departments or Information Technology or Information Systems Planning AND In Keyword, Subject/Descriptor, or Title fields: management or governance or strategy or strategic planning or procurement or e-govern!

Dates: 1996–Current

We made a second search of the same databases, with the addition of the database PsycINFO, using "best practices" in the Keyword, Subject, or Title fields. Several themes emerged from the literature, which we discuss under separate headings below.

Public Sector IT Investment and Productivity

There are many more private sector studies on IT investment than there are public sector studies. The public sector studies are consistent, however, in concluding that IT investment pays off. Studies at local, county, state, and federal levels all show that public sector IT investment has a direct, positive effect on productivity and performance (Brown, 2001; Brown, O'Toole, and Brudney, 1998; Heintze and Bretschneider, 2000; Lee and Perry, 2002; Lehr and Lichtenberg, 1996 [cited in Lee and Perry, 2002]). A study of IT investment by state governments, based on data from all 50 states, showed a direct, positive effect on economic productivity, as measured by Gross State Product (GSP). This held true whether IT investment was measured in financial terms or by a

84

performance index based on total computer processing power (Lee and Perry, 2002).

Leadership

The active attention and support of top management for IT has been found to be critical to its success, across organizations of all sizes in both public and private sectors. In studies at the local and county levels, researchers found that management support and leadership had a direct, positive influence on the commitment of employees to IT projects, organizational performance after IT implementation, and the realization of expected benefits from IT projects (Brown, O'Toole, and Brudney, 1998; Heintze and Bretschneider, 2000). A study of Fortune 1000 companies and government agencies found a significant positive relationship between top management leadership and the sophistication of IT infrastructure (Ravichandran and Rai, 2000). In a collection of small studies of IT failures in public agencies in California, one of the most consistent conclusions was that when new software is adopted, management support for the application and the employees learning to use it is essential (Northrop, 2002). (The small studies described in this paper were student projects assigned over a six-year period by a single professor; conceivably the student conclusions were influenced by the views of the professor.)

Private sector studies have found that senior management support, championship, and commitment is critical for IT assimilation (Armstrong and Sambamurthy, 1999), for meeting procurement goals in large organizations (Avery, 2001), and for successful implementation of IT security (Internal Auditor, 1997). Similarly, a study of tens of thousands of software projects concluded that there is most success where senior executives have a clear vision of the goals of a project and communicate their vision throughout the company (Ware, May 2001).

Management Styles

In a study of IT investment in all 50 states of the United States, Lee and Perry compared four different management structures: a single CIO, an Information Resources Management (IRM) commission (typically made up of top managers in state agencies with a stake in IT), a combination of the two, or no formal IT management functions at all. They found that states with a single CIO got a better return on their investment (in terms of economic benefits to the state) than states with any other kind of formal structure; in addition they found that states with an IRM commission alone did no better than states with no formal IT management functions.

The primary role of business units or agencies in determining the goals of IT is emphasized in several studies. A program to introduce IT in the Charlotte-Mecklenberg Police Department began with several rounds of interviews and focus groups to find out what kind of information officers and other employees thought they needed in order to do their work better; once the resulting IT system was implemented, between half and three-quarters of officers perceived a threefold or better improvement in performance, efficiency, call-response, and problem-solving productivity (Brown, 2001). Several studies emphasize the importance of letting business units or agencies who will use the IT set the agenda by proposing initiatives, controlling the financing, and being continuously involved in the planning and testing of IT projects (Radosevich, 2001; Internal Auditor, 1997; Kiely, 1997; Northrop, 2002; Avery, 2001).

One additional frequent observation is that in planning and managing IT projects, the adoption of clear, short-term sub-goals within each project, with regular testing and early, frequent involvement of users, is an important factor in the successful completion of large projects (Ware, May 2001; Internal Auditor, 1997; Radosevich, 1999).

Strategic Planning

Several studies of strategic planning for IT emphasize the importance of committing sufficient resources to the planning process, in terms of time, money, and the personal attention of top managers (Management Review, 1999; Ramanujam, Venkatraman, and Camillus, 1986; Ware, Nov. 2001). A large study of Fortune 1000 companies and government agencies found that using an integrated planning strategy that makes use of all identified success factors is far more likely to succeed than the implementation of a single tool or management practice (Ravichandran and Rai, 2000).

While not many organizations make effective use of metrics in their planning, the use of appropriate metrics has been found to be an important success factor across firms of all sizes; in general the collection and analysis of relevant information is an important factor (Dean and Sharfman, 1996).

Two negative factors in strategic planning have been identified: the degree of resistance to planning, or anti-planning bias, within an organization (Ramanujam, Venkatraman, and Camillus, 1986), and the extent to which politics, defined as "intentional acts of influence in the service of individual rather than organizational goals," plays a role (Dean and Sharfman, 1996).

Procurement and Outsourcing

There is some consensus on several recommendations having to do with procurement practices and outsourcing. A case study of IT procurement in three large firms recommends having a central, global system for keeping track of IT expenditures (Avery, 2001). Two studies found that involving people with both business and technical expertise in procurement and outsourcing decisions is better than either group operating alone (Avery, 2001; Lacity and Willcocks, 1998). In a study of outsourcing in 40 U.S. and U.K. corporations, Lacity and Willcocks found that outsourcing selectively is more effective in reducing cost than either total outsourcing or no outsourcing at all. Also, short-term contracts using multiple vendors, with detailed fee-for-service agreements, result in greater cost reductions than long-term, open-ended contracts. Finally, all of these findings seem to hold regardless of the size of the IT function within an organization (Lacity and Wilcocks, 1998).

Bibliography

Armstrong, C. P., and V. Sambamurthy. 1999. Information Technology Assimilation in Firms: The Influence of Senior Leadership and IT Infrastructures. *Information Systems Research*, 10(4), 304–327.

Avery, S. 2001. IT Procurement "Best Practices" Series (special report; cover story). *Purchasing*, 130(12), 23–28.

Bailey, W. J., R. Masson, and R. Raeside. 1998. Choosing Successful Technology Development Partners: A Best-Practice Model. *International Journal of Technology Management*, 15(1), 124–138.

Best Practices in IT Controls. 1997. *Internal Auditor*, 54(4), 12.

Bikson, T. K. 1986. Understanding the Implementation of Office Technology. In Robert Kraut (ed.), *Technology and the Transformation of White Collar Work*, Hillsdale, NJ: Erlbaum Associates, 155-176. (Also available from RAND as N-2619-NSF.)

Bikson, T. K. 1998. Managing Digital Documents: Technology Challenges and Institutional Responses. In *Proceedings of the International Conference of the Round Table on Archives*, Stockholm, Sweden: International Council on Archives, September 1998. (The French version is available as "Gestion des Documents Numeriques: Defis Technologiques et Reponses des Institutions.")

Bikson, T. K., S. G. Cohen, and D. Mankin, 1998. Teams and Information Technology: Creating Value Through Knowledge. In E. Sundstrom (ed.), *Supporting Work Team Effectiveness: Creating the Context for High Performance*, San Francisco: Jossey Bass, 1998, 215-245.

Bikson, T. K., and J. D. Eveland. 1996. Groupware Implementation: Reinvention in the Sociotechnical Frame. In *Proceedings of the Conference on Computer-Supported Cooperative Work*, New York: Association for Computing Machinery, 1996, 428-437. (Also available as RAND Reprint RP-703.)

Bikson, T. K., and E. J. Frinking. 1993. *Preserving the Present: Toward Viable Electronic Records*, Den Haag: Sdu Publishers, (Parts of this book are available as RAND Reprint RP-257.)

Bikson, T. K., B. A. Gutek, and D. Mankin. 1987. *Implementing Computerized Procedures in Office Settings: Influences and Outcomes*. Santa Monica, CA: RAND, R-3077-NSF.

Birge, E. M. 1997. Managing the Decentralized IT Organization. *Information Systems Management*, 14(3), 77–82.

Botterman, M., T. K. Bikson, S. Bosman, J. Cave, E. Frinking, and V. dePous. 2000. *Public Information Provision in the Digital Age: Implementation and Effects of the US Freedom of Information Act*, Den Haag: Sdu Publishers.

Brancheau, J. C., B. D. Janz, and J. C. Wetherbe. 1996. Key Issues in Information Systems Management: 1994-1995 SIM Delphi Results. *MIS Quarterly*, 20, 225–242.

Broadbent, M., P. Weill, and D. Clair. 1999. The Implications of Information Technology Infrastructure for Business Process Redesign. *MIS Quarterly,* 23(2), 159-182.

Brown, M. M. 2001. The Benefits and Costs of Information Technology Innovations: An Empirical Assessment of a Local Government Agency. *Public Performance & Management Review,* 24(4), 351–366.

Brown, M. M., and J. L. Brudney. 1998. Public Sector Information Technology Initiatives: Implications for Programs of Public Administration. *Administration & Society,* 30(4), 421-442.

Brown, M. M., L. J. O'Toole Jr., and J. L. Brudney. 1998. Implementing Information Technology in Government: An Empirical Assessment of the Role of Local Partnerships. *Journal of Public Administration Research and Theory,* 8(4), 499–525.

California Franchise Tax Board. 1998. *Performance Based Procurement: Another Model for California.* Paper presented at John F. Kennedy School of Government, Harvard University.

California State Auditor, Bureau of State Audits. 2001. *Information Technology: The State Needs to Improve the Leadership and Management of Its Information Technology Efforts.* Sacramento, CA: Report No. 2000–118.

California State University Center for Public Dispute Resolution. 2002. *Outcomes Report: Results of a Focus Group Study for the Department of Information Technology,* Sacramento, CA.

Campbell, D. T. 1975. Degrees of Freedom and the Case Study, *Comparative Political Studies,* 8, 178–193.

Chen, L., and K. S. Soliman. 2002. Managing IT Outsourcing: A Value-Driven Approach to Outsourcing Using Application Service Providers. *Logistics Information Management,* 15(3), 180–191.

Cohen, Susan G., and D. E. Bailey. 1997. What Makes Teams Work: Group Effectiveness Research from the Shop Floor to the Executive Suite. *Journal of Management,* 23(3), 239–290.

Comeau-Kirschner, C. 1999. Most IT Projects Prove Inefficient. *Management Review,* 88(1), 7.

Cooper, R., and R. W. Zmud. 1990. Information Technology Implementation Research: A Technological Diffusion Approach. *Management Science,* 36(2), 123–139.

Cooper, R. B. 2000. Information Technology Development Creativity: A Case Study of Attempted Radical Change. *MIS Quarterly*, 24(2), 245–276.

Currie, W. L. 1995. Organizational Structure and the Use of Information Technology: Preliminary Findings of a Survey in the Private and Public Sector. *International Journal of Information Management*, 16(1), 51–64.

Dean, J. W., Jr., and M. P. Sharfman. 1996. Does Decision Process Matter? A Study of Strategic Decision-Making Effectiveness. *The Academy of Management Journal*, 39(2), 368–396.

Department of Information Technology. 2001. *Capability Assessment Report: Report to the Legislature in Response to the Supplemental Report of the 2000 Budget Act.* Sacramento, CA.

Department of Information Technology. 2002. *The Statewide Information Technology Strategic Plan* (draft), Version 13. Sacramento, CA.

Department of Information Technology. 1998. *1998 Annual Report,* Sacramento, CA.

Department of Information Technology. 1999. *1999 Annual Report.* Sacramento, CA.

Department of Information Technology. 2000. *2000 Annual Report.* Sacramento, CA.

Earl, M., and D. Feeny. 2000. Opinion: How to Be a CEO for the Information Age. *MIT Sloan Management Review*, 41(2), 11–23.

Earl, M. J., and J. L. Sampler. 1998. Market Management to Transform the IT Organization. *MIT Sloan Management Review*, 39(4), 10–17.

Enterprise Systems Subcommittee of the Information Technology Coordinating Council. 1997. *Report from the Enterprise Systems Subcommittee of the Information Technology Coordinating Council on State of California Enterprise Systems Strategy.* Sacramento, CA.

Garud, R., A. Kumaraswamy, and P. Nayyar. 1998. Real Options or Fool's Gold? Perspective Makes the Difference. *Academy of Management Review*, 23(2), 212–214.

Goodhue, D. 1995. Understanding User Evaluations of Information Systems. *Management Science*, 41(12), 1827–1844.

Gurbaxani, V., K. Kraemer, and N. Vitalari. 1997. Note: An Economic Analysis of IS Budgets. *Management Science*, 43(12), 1745–1755.

Hackman, J. Richard. 1998. Why Teams Don't Work. In R. Scott Tindale and Linda Heath (eds.), *Theory and Research on Small Groups,* New York: Plenum Press, 245-267.

Hann, J., and R. Weber. 1996. Information Systems Planning: A Model and Empirical Tests. *Management Science*, 42(7), 1043–1064.

90

Hartwick, J., and H. Barki. 1994. Explaining the Role of User Participation in Information System Use. *Management Science,* 40(4), 440–464.

Heintze, T., and S. Bretschneider. 2000. Information Technology And Restructuring in Public Organizations: Does Adoption of Information Technology Affect Organizational Structures, Communications, and Decision Making? *Journal of Public Administration Research and Theory,* 10(4), 801–830.

Hersen, M., and D. Barlow. 1976. *Single Case Experimental Designs: Strategies for Studying Behavior*, New York: Pergamon Press..

Hildreth, P., C. Kimble, and P. Wright. 2000. Communities of Practice in the Distributed International Environment. *Journal of Knowledge Management,* 4(1), 27–38.

Hill, E.G. 1998. *State Should Employ "Best Practices" on Information Technology Projects.* Sacramento, CA: Legislative Analyst's Office.

ITCC Task Force on Information Technology Staff Recruitment and Retention. 1998. *Information Technology Staff Recruitment And Retention: Protecting and Improving the Delivery of Services to California.*

Kiely, T. 1997. "Information Technology—Making Collaboration Work. *Harvard Business Review,* 75(1), 10–11.

Lacity, M. C., and L. P. Willcocks. 1998. An Empirical Investigation of Information Technology Sourcing Practices: Lessons from Experience. *MIS Quarterly*, 22(3), 363–408.

Larwood, L., C. M. Falbe, M. P. Kriger, and P. Miesing. 1995. Structure and Meaning of Organizational Vision. *The Academy of Management Journal,* 38(3), 740–769.

Lee, G., and J. L. Perry. 2002. Are Computers Boosting Productivity? A Test of the Paradox in State Governments. *Journal of Public Administration Research and Theory*, 12(1), 77–102.

Lee, H. K., and D. D. Dea. 1997. Unleashing the Power of Your Web Site. *Association Management,* 49(13), 39–46.

Lefebvre, L. A., R. Mason, and E. Lefebvre. 1997. The Influence Prism in SMEs: The Power of CEO's Perceptions on Technology Policy and Its Organizational Impacts. *Management Science,* 43(6), 856–878.

Legislative Analyst's Office. 1996. *State Information Technology: An Update.* Sacramento, CA.

Legislative Analyst's Office. 1997. *Analysis of 1997-1998 Budget Bill.* Sacramento, CA.

Legislative Analyst's Office. 1999. *Analysis of 1999-2000 Budget Bill.* Sacramento, CA.

Legislative Analyst's Office. 2001. *Analysis of 2001-2002 Budget Bill.* Sacramento, CA.

Lehr, W., and F. R. Lichtenberg. 1996. Computer Use And Productivity Growth in Federal Government Agencies 1987 to 1992. Working Paper no. 5616. Cambridge, MA: National Bureau of Economic Research.

Little Hoover Commission. 2000. *Better Government: Engineering Technology-Enhanced Government.* Sacramento, CA.

MacCormack, A. 2001. Product-Development Practices That Work: How Internet Companies Build Software. *MIT Sloan Management Review,* 42(2), 75–84.

Mayor, T. 1997. Ensured Stability. *CIO,* 10(19), 62–68.

McCampbell, A. S., L. M. Clare, and S. H. Gitters. 1999. Knowledge Management: The New Challenge for the 21st Century. *Journal of Knowledge Management,* 3(3), 172–179.

Miller, D. 1987. Strategy Making and Structure: Analysis and Implications for Performance. *The Academy of Management Journal,* 30(1), 7–32.

Nambisan, S., R. Agarwal, and M. Tanniru. 1999. Organizational Mechanisms for Enhancing User Innovation in Information Technology. *MIS Quarterly,* 23(3), 365–395.

Northrop, A. 2002. Lessons for Managing Information Technology in the Public Sector. *Social Science Computer Review,* 20(2), 194–205.

Philip, G., and M. E. Booth. 1998. A New Six 'S' Framework on the Relationship Between the Role of Information Systems (IS) and Competencies in 'IS' Management. *Journal of Business Research,* 51, 233–247.

Radosevich, L. 1999. Measuring Up. *CIO,* 12(23), 52–54, 56.

Ramanujam, V., N. Venkatraman, and J. C. Camillus. 1986. Multi-Objective Assessment of Effectiveness of Strategic Planning: A Discriminant Analysis Approach, *The Academy of Management Journal,* 29(2), 347–372.

Ravichandran, T., and A. Rai. 2000. Quality Management in Systems Development: An Organizational System Perspective. *MIS Quarterly,* 24(3), 381–415.

Reich, B. H., and I. Benbasat. 1996. Measuring the Linkage Between Business and Information Technology Objectives. *MIS Quarterly,* 20(1), 55–81.

Rocheleau, B. 2000. Prescriptions for Public-Sector Information Management: A Review, Analysis, and Critique. *American Review of Public Administration,* 30(4), 414–435.

Rockart, J. F., M. J. Earl, and J. W. Ross. 1996. Eight Imperatives for the New IT Organization. *MIT Sloan Management Review,* 38(1), 4355.

Schilling, M. A. 1998. Technological Lockout: An Integrative Model of the Economic And Strategic Factors Driving Technology Success and Failure. *Academy of Management Review*, 23(2), 267–284.

Segars, A. H., and V. Grover. 1998. Strategic Information Systems Planning Success: An Investigation of the Construct and Its Measurement. *MIS Quarterly*, 22(2), 139–163.

Segars, A. H., and V. Grover. 1999. Profiles of Strategic Information Systems Planning. *Information Systems Research*, 10(3), 199–232.

Sethi, V., and W. King, 1994. Development of Measures to Assess the Extent to Which an Information Technology Application Provides Competitive Advantage. *Management Science*, 40(12), 1601–1627.

Simmons, C. W., and A. Bugarin. 1999. *Building a Skilled State Information and Technology Workforce*. California Research Bureau, California State Library, CRB-99-007.

Stasz, C., T. K. Bikson, J. D. Eveland, and J. Adams. *Assessing Benefits of the U.S. Forest Service's Geographic Information System: Research Design*, Santa Monica, CA: RAND, N-3245-USDAFS, 1991.

Stasz, C., T. K. Bikson, J. D. Eveland, and B. Mittman. *Information Technology in the U.S. Forest Service: An Assessment of Late Stage Implementation*, Santa Monica, CA: RAND, R-3908-USDAFS, 1990.

State of California. 1994. *Report of the Task Force on Government Technology Policy and Procurement*. Sacramento, CA: Governor's Office of Planning and Research.

State of California. 1995. *Statutes of 1995* (chapter 508), SB 1, Alquist.

Stephenson, P. 2000. Standards or "Best-Practices"—Conflicting Interests: Approaches to Information Protection. *Information Systems Security*, 9(3), 5–10.

Storck, J., and P. A. Hill. 2000. Knowledge Diffusion Through "Strategic Communities." *MIT Sloan Management Review*, 41(2), 63–74.

Swanson, E. B. 1994. Information Systems Innovation Among Organizations. *Management Science*, 40(9), 1069–1092.

Trist, E., and K. Bamforth, 1951. Some Social and Psychological Consequences of the Longwall Method of Coal Getting. *Human Relations*, 4, 3–38.

U. S. General Accounting Office, Accounting and Information Management Division. 1998. *Measuring Performance and Demonstrating Results of Information Technology Investments*. Washington, DC: GAO/AIMD-98-99.

Venkatraman, N. 1997. Beyond Outsourcing: Managing IT Resources as a Value Center, *MIT Sloan Management Review*, 38(3), 51–64.

Voorhees, W. R. 2002. How and Why to Strategically Finance IT Projects. *Government Finance Review*, 18(2), 42–43.

Walker, D. 2001. *Human Capital: Meeting the Governmentwide High-Risk Challenge.* Washington, DC: General Accounting Office, GAO-01-357T.

Ware, L. C. 2001. By the Numbers: Managing Software Projects. *CIO,* 14(14), 34–39.

Ware, L. C. 2001. By the Numbers: Retain Your Top IT Talent, *CIO,* 15(3), 30–33.

Ware, L. C. 2001. By the Numbers: Simplifying Your Computing Environment. *CIO,* 14(22), 30–35.

Ware, L. C. (2001). By the Numbers: Measuring IT Alignment, *CIO,* 14(12), 32–37.

Yin, R. K. 1984. *Case Study Research: Design and Methods,* Newbury Park, CA: Sage Publications.